divine CONVERSATIONS

Divine CONVERSATIONS

Details of some stories have been changed to protect the identities of the persons involved.

Paperback ISBN 978-1-7349028-0-8

Published by Joyful & Free Publishing Co.
Cover and book design by Kayla J. Nelson

Kathy is a woman who loves the LORD deeply. By spending a few moments with her, you will know that this woman knows Jesus. She is wise and insightful, gifted by the Spirit to share wisdom and insight in her writing.

In Divine Conversations, she expands on conversations that take place between people in the Bible and God. As she shares her knowledge of the scripture you come to see more clearly the love of God, the truth of His Word, and the impact of our conversations with Him.

The lessons are easy to follow and understand. In the digging deeper sections, she asks questions to help you make the lesson more applicable to your life. There are also great group discussion questions that will lead to deep conversations with those whom you are sharing this study.

While this study is meant to be done with a group, it can also be done individually. Divine Conversations will encourage you to have deep conversations with God, and to listen to His voice as He speaks with you.

-- **Bethany Christensen**, Sammy's small group leader

"If you are curious as to whether the Holy Spirit still speaks to God's people or how to connect with Him, Divine Conversations is a one-of-a-kind study for you!

In each chapter, Kathy Schwanke shares stories of answered prayer in her life and leads us in exploring conversations people have with God in the Bible, including Jesus Himself! She challenges us to examine our own hearts and prayer lives while motivating us to pursue more faith-filled conversations with God.

She includes skillfully crafted study questions which aid application to our unique individual circumstances. Ultimately, we learn to hear the holy whispers of the Spirit of God. There is not much of a chance that you can complete this study and be the same person you were when you began!"

--**Pennie Bixler**, Founder of Sammy's Inc., Sammy's Bible study leader, Biblical Counselor at Faith Community Church, Hudson, WI

"Several of us did a Bible study together using the study guide, Divine Conversations, written by Kathy Schwanke. This study was very helpful in our sharing of personal experiences with the Lord. It was also valuable in encouraging private journaling. It was a great balance of scripture and personal testimony. It led us as a group into good sharing and prayer times. The Prayer Prompts were especially helpful. Overall it was one of the best Bible studies I have done."

--**Judy Fox**, Participant, North Springs Church, Lino Lakes, MN

First, thank you to Jesus.
Your word is the most beautiful light, and my greatest delight!

To my husband of 36 years, Dale, and our blessed family: for loving Jesus with me and allowing me to share your stories for His glory!

To my daughter Kayla for making this book pretty with your gift of design.

To my Mom who initiated my love for the Bible and who loves to study my material with her friends.

To my friends who have dug into scripture with me, you know who you are!

To my pastors who saw my gifts and gave me opportunity to use them.

To the SAMMY'S INC board, including Emily Staples, for initially commissioning me to write this study, and then gifting it back to me to go out into the wider world.

To the reader who seeks to go deeper with God:
I pray you have many divine conversations as you go light your world!

table OF CONTENTS

INTRODUCTION 9

1. **ABRAHAM**: *believes & receives* 13

2. **JACOB**: *wrestled & revived* 29

3. **HANNAH**: *fervent & overflowing* 45

4. **JONAH**: *surrender & salvation* 61

5. **MOSES**: *intercedes & advances* 75

6. **NEHEMIAH**: *zealous & faithful* 91

7. **SOLOMON**: *power & presence & pleasure* 105

8. **ZECHARIAH'S** *"AHA!"* 121

9. **JESUS**: *broken to fill* 137

10. **MARY**: *favored & blessed* 151

GROUP DISCUSSION QUESTIONS 171

RESOURCES 193

NOTES 201

ABOUT THE AUTHOR 203

When you are done, please tuck this book in a place where you can return to read your penned prayers in the years to come.

Perhaps every new year, you could return to it, and watch the progress that the Lord makes in your faith.

Recording your prayers and praises is extremely valuable for your faith, and of those who come behind you.

INTRODUCTION

& how to use this book

Greetings Dear Sisters,

I am so honored to be a part of your journey with Jesus! I pray that your prayer life will be set on fire through ***divine* CONVERSATIONS**.

You may have heard it said, *"prayer changes things."*

The saying is true! In every divine conversation you will study in this book, you will see the encounters with God bring transformation to the lives of His people. Not only growth and victory in the person God is communicating with, but for multitudes touched by His grace!

Expect God to move mountains and part seas through your prayer life!

It's important that you learn to lay your prayers on the foundation of God's promises. You'll have opportunity to do that in this study.

As the writing of divine CONVERSATIONS progressed, a few themes emerged. You might notice that encounters with God always brought about movement, which often resulted in hearts bursting forth in praise.

There is also an emphasis on our longings. You'll see the way God gives them to us and uses them to fuel movement in our lives.

The refining wilderness theme recurs often as well. Look for glimpses of what God is writing in your own story, even during the dryest wilderness times.

Expect to see your heart through the eyes of God. In doing so, you will be brought nearer to His heart because of His fervent, unconditional love for you. He wants us to want Him, and He knows exactly what to do to get us where He wants us -- closer to Him through prayer!

Record Your Encounters With God

This study leaves a page at the end of each week for you to pen a prayer to God. There are prompts with scripture to guide you. You have freedom of course to completely go "off topic" with whatever is burning on your heart. I suggest dating your prayers so you can remember more clearly when you look back.

After you are finished, you will have recorded more than ten intimate and personal prayers. Plan on looking back at them a year from now to see how the Lord has answered you.

In his book, *Soul Print*, Mark Batterson suggests that we are stewards of our memories. Your encounters with God -- when they are recorded and shared with others . . . your children, your co-workers, and your friends, will be used to build and bless God's people. Your encounters will encourage others to seek Him.

Before you start:

- Consider keeping a separate journal or spiral bound index-cards, and write out scriptures that are meaningful to you as you go through this study.

- Have a set of colored pencils for highlighting and coloring. May as well make your study time pretty!

- The lessons each take about 35-45 minutes if you read, look up scripture, and answer the questions. In the back of the book, I've included a resource page including recommended songs* and suggested reading for going deeper in each week's topic. To get the most out of this study, even setting aside an extra 15 minutes for listening to a song and coloring or doodling your thoughts will enhance your experience and grow your personal intimacy with God.

**Music is a gracious gift to us from God, as it cements truth into our hearts more securely.*

Suggested use of this Bible study:

You will most certainly benefit from reading **Divine CONVERSATIONS** on your own. However, we always glean the most from study in the context of gathering together with others.

If you have questions or would like to learn more about Kathy's ministry, you can find her at www.kathyschwanke.com

The book is designed to:

- Read ahead on your own.
- Follow along during a large group teaching time.
- Foster small-group discussions with the discussion questions found at the back of the book.

The sections titled **Digging Deeper** offer work for you to do on your own to enhance your bible study experience. You should do the work before you come to the meeting so you can offer your unique insight to the group discussion.

Large Group Teaching:

As you gather with the large group, you might have a time of teaching to go over the previous week's work, with additional stories and comments from the study leader. I suggest varying your teachers in order to give opportunity for those interested to practice teaching. My speaking ministry began through such opportunities in my local church and I'm extremely grateful!

Small Group Discussion:

I love how the Holy Spirit works mightily among us when we pour over His word *together*. Because of this, I pray a good chunk of time will be dedicated to small group conversation. I've included discussion questions in the workbook at the end of each chapter.

1

ABRAHAM

believes & receives

When Abram was ninety-nine years old
the Lord appeared to Abram and said to him,
"I am God Almighty; walk before me, and be blameless, that
I may make my covenant between me and you, and may
multiply you greatly."

Then Abram fell on his face.
Genesis 17:1-3a

How Does God Work His Will?

Worry. Fear. All throughout scripture we are exhorted *"Do NOT."*
"Do not worry."
"Do not fear."
"Do not be anxious."

God knows we will.

The exhortations are there for our encouragement, so that when our emotions rage, they can be signposts that we need to seek the Lord.

You might know that God has unique promises for your life, but you are nowhere near living the life you thought you were created for. How do you navigate disappointment? How do you endure long seasons of waiting?

What do you do when you are overwhelmed by the size of something, either good or bad? Being in the presence of the King can overwhelm us, and so can our own inabilities.

Sickness, bankruptcy, infertility, divorce, rebellious children, drug addiction, mental illness – all of these can bring great anxiety into our lives. We can respond with or without God. When we go without God, we can spiral into our own desolate places, into depression or sickness. Or we can take matters into our own hands and bring great distress into our lives.

The better option is to choose to go to our knees . . . or maybe our face... before the only Source we know to have the power to help us.

Has desperation driven you to your knees?
Have you found yourself "face down" in the carpet
due to something you cannot control?

____

____

____

____

____

We've all heard the saying, *"Ashes to ashes, dust to dust."* Usually the lips that have uttered the phrase are saying goodbyes to a loved one while standing graveside, staring at a mound of earth. This is the place where we remember our beginnings and our endings.

Many things in scripture begin from dust. A glance through scenes in the Gospels will show people falling, knees to the dusty ground, at the feet of Jesus. It is at that very place where we will see the power of God come in and make beautiful things out of dust.

God Speaks

I couldn't take notes fast enough. My heart was on fire as the speaker poured truth from her mouth like a firehose. My heart ached to have such wisdom and faith flow from my own lips.

As she continued to relay stories of God's work in and through her life, I leaned in harder. She'd shared Jesus with a homeless man in the skyway in Minneapolis. I couldn't imagine having that kind of courage with my new faith.

Somehow during the evening session of the retreat words dropped into my heart -- words I sensed were from God. Shocking words, actually. "You will do this one day."

I knew He meant speaking. My reply to God was, "Okay, but You have a lot of work to do."

After my one and only speaking experience in tenth grade english, I'd determined after sitting down at my desk, that I would NEVER do that again! I felt as if I were melting like the Wicked Witch of the West in The Wizard of Oz upon being doused by a bucket of water.

Me? Shy, insecure, fearful-of-being-known farmgirl?

I received the words as God's even though I was not sure if they were from Him. I assumed so, because as far as I knew, it was not coming from a desire within my own heart.

It was 1997.

Little did I know the journey would include taking many steps of obedience into very scary places.

I began "ministry" by teaching Sunday school to children. As my children grew, I stepped up grade by grade. Sometimes I was with our firstborn, Kayla's class. Other times I was teaching our son Ethan's class, two grades younger.

Three years after hearing the call from God to "do this one day," I fell into a pit of anxiety and depression. I knew it was spiritual warfare and I was terrified. I struggled in the darkness for several years in varying degrees, and the Lord delivered me over time. On one of the darkest nights of a six week season of insomnia, when I was being tormented by my faith failure, I heard another phrase drop into my heart the same way it had at the retreat in 1997.

"You will lead women in triumphal procession." I knew what God meant, as I'd just read 2 Corinthians 2:14 which says, "But thanks be to God, who in Christ always leads us in triumphal procession, and through us spreads the fragrance of the knowledge of him everywhere."

I understood Him to be saying, "I will lead women to experience My victory through your ministry."

A few years later I understood what God had allowed the affliction for -- at least to some degree as I began to mentor and pray with several women and girls who were struggling with emotional issues like anorexia, cutting, and depression.

Because I'd endured the war, I could fight on behalf of others.

When Kayla started highschool, I joined the youth group ministry team where I shepherded the ninth and tenth grade girls. I was given a few opportunities to address the youth group. And I did it scared.

One of my messages included bringing an oil lamp in to depict our hearts upon being born again into the family of God. I chose a boy to assist me in lighting the lamp. When it came time for him to man the firestick, I paused to shift attention on the lamp. He couldn't get it to work. He tried for several minutes, but the cloth wick would not receive the flame.

It was a flop.

How I melted at the thought that I'd not only failed to prep well by testing the lamp, but I'd also caused the poor boy to suffer humiliation in front of a large crowd of peers.

One boy approached me on my way out to thank me for the message, but naturally I thought he was doing it out of sympathy. I left melting in shame.

Upon becoming an empty nester, I was asked to start a Women's Ministry. I'd already been leading Bible studies with women for ten years while serving the youth. My hunger for God's word and love of teaching continued to increase. Eventually I taught our Women's Sunday School class and loved it.

I also spoke at half a dozen of our women's retreats and ministry events. Slowly I was gaining confidence.

The "one day" finally came in 2014 when my mom asked her Pastor's wife if they would invite me to speak to their women's gathering.

Again, I was stepping into what God had called me to do with fear but also with faith in the words I'd heard God speak to me. As of this writing, I have five years of consistent speaking engagements. I still fall to my knees or face down in the carpet to pray for God to give me the words He wants me to speak as I prepare.

But I'm happy to report that I've finally gotten over the melting, as I've grown in the trusting.

God is not looking at our performance as much as He's looking at who we are becoming.

God Promises

When God called Abram, He called him *"out of his country and kindred and father's house"* into a land that God *"would show him."* This calling came with an initial promise, *"I will bless you and make your name great, so that you will be a blessing."* (Genesis 12:1-2)

Abram responded to the call of God, and leaving everything behind, he took his wife Sarai and his nephew Lot with him to follow God. Abram went through a "wilderness" period for roughly 24 years where God taught Him about God, *and about Abram,* through many moves, fears, conflicts and battles.

In God's sovereign wisdom, He has designed the wilderness experience to bring things which are hidden in the darkness of our souls to the surface. Abram's life exposed a mixture of worship and sin as he sojourned. When Abram set up his tent, he'd build an altar and worship the Lord. When a famine moved them to Egypt, he was fearful that the Egyptians would kill him and take his beautiful wife Sarai, so he asked her to say she was his sister – *instead of fulfilling his delegated responsibility as husband, to protect her, he hid behind her lie – more than once.*

Lot and Abram's herdsmen were having conflict over the rich land. Abram showed trust in the Lord when he let Lot choose which way he wanted to go with his herds, and Abram would go the other way. He yielded preference to avoid conflict.

God showed up again in Genesis 15, promising Abram descendants from his own body as numerous as the stars. God made a covenant with him on the basis of sacrifice. Abram gathered and cut in half, a three-year-old heifer, a three –year-old goat, and a three-year-old ram. He also brought a turtle dove and a young pigeon. He laid them out on the ground, and as night fell, a deep sleep fell on Abram. A dreadful great darkness fell upon him, and the Lord spoke to him, telling him about the journey his offspring would take in the future to the land of Egypt, and through a season of oppression. Finally, he assured him of their exodus from Egypt with great possessions. It would be the fourth generation that would take the land promised to Abram upon his initial call to leave home and family.

After God's sacrificial covenant with Abram, Sarai remained childless, and "got a bright idea" one day, to offer her personal servant, Hagar, to Abram. She thought this would solve the problem. After all, the promise hadn't *directly* mentioned her . . . So of course Abram obliged. Ishmael was born to Hagar, but instead of the joy Sarai anticipated, there was strife and conflict between the two women.

There is much to glean from Abraham, Sarah and Hagar's story, but for this study, we are going to continue at the time when Ishmael was around twelve years old.

Please read Genesis 17:1-8 and 15-17

> When Abram was ninety-nine years old the Lord appeared to Abram and said to him, "I am God Almighty; walk before me, and be blameless, 2 that I may make my covenant between me and you, and may multiply you greatly." 3 Then Abram fell on his face. And God said to him, 4 "Behold, my covenant is with you, and you shall be the father of a multitude of nations. 5 No longer shall your name be called Abram, but your name shall be Abraham, for I have made you the father of a multitude of nations. 6 I will make you exceedingly fruitful, and I will make you into nations, and kings shall come from you. 7 And I will establish my covenant between me and you and your offspring after you throughout their generations for an everlasting covenant, to be God to you and to your offspring after you. 8 And I will give to you and to your offspring after you the land of your sojournings, all the land of Canaan, for an everlasting possession, and I will be their God."
>
> 15 And God said to Abraham, "As for Sarai your wife, you shall not call her name Sarai, but Sarah shall be her name. 16 I will bless her, and moreover, I will give you a son by her. I will bless her, and she shall become nations; kings of peoples shall come from her." 17 Then Abraham fell on his face and laughed and said to himself, "Shall a child be born to a man who is a hundred years old? Shall Sarah, who is ninety years old, bear a child?"

The Lord showed up one day in Abram's ninety-ninth year and spoke to Abram stating:
1. "I am God Almighty."
2 "Walk before me and be blameless."
3. "I will make a covenant with you and multiply you greatly."

Can you feel what Abram felt? ***Whoa! Wait, WHAT?*** How does a man who has lied about his wife and who impregnated his wife's servant, respond to a mighty God calling him to *be blameless and multiply at the age of ninety-nine*?

What does Abram do? He falls on his face! By this time in his life, roughly twenty-four years after God promised to make him into a great nation, *he knows he cannot be blameless.*

God seems to overlook Abram's humble posture, as it seems He went right on speaking. His next word was *"Behold"* In case you haven't noticed in scripture; this word shows up a lot. How often outside of scripture does anyone use the term "*behold?"*

We might use the word, "LOOK!" as a call to greater attention and emphasis.

Let's paraphrase: "LOOK, Abram, My covenant is with you, and I'm changing your name. I'm adding an *"ah"* right smack in the middle of it. No longer will you be Abram. You will now be called Abr**AH**am.

According to the site, "Hebrew For Christians," the "H" in Hebrew stands for the breath of God, or the Spirit of God. The name the Hebrews used for God, Yahweh, actually sounded like a breath when they dared speak it. It was only ever spoken with extreme reverence. Additionally, in the name for God, *El-oh-him*, the "oh" in the middle means "one that swears by an oath" which fits well with the fact that God is establishing a covenant to secure His forever family.

What we are witnessing here is nothing short of a holy union, a sacred covenantal bond between God and Abraham, including Sarai, as He changes her name to Sar**AH** a few verses later.

Abram's name means *"exalted father*" and God changed his name to Abraham, which means, *"Father of a multitude."* Sarai's name, meaning *"Princess"* was changed to Sarah, meaning: *"Princess of many."*

In our culture, upon entering into covenant with our husbands, we change our family-identifying name. So it was with God, Abraham and Sarah. God made a familial covenant prior to His promised fruitfulness.

Read Genesis 17:15-17 again.

> 15 And God said to Abraham, "As for Sarai your wife, you shall not call her name Sarai, but Sarah shall be her name. 16 I will bless her, and moreover, I will give you a son by her. I will bless her, and she shall become nations; kings of peoples shall come from her." 17 Then Abraham fell on his face and laughed and said to himself, "Shall a child be born to a man who is a hundred years old? Shall Sarah, who is ninety years old, bear a child?"

This might be the introduction to God's sense of humor. Picture these scenes in the midst of something so entirely serious as a Covenant between God and man. The weight of this scene is truly the foundation of our study; it's the very premise of us being here today, seeking to grow in our communication with God.

Evidentially, after having fallen on his face the first time, Abraham had stood to his feet, because we find him falling on his face again here, just a few verses later. Only this time, it's not only in the spirit of humility, but seemingly in a *spirit of hilarity!* Now it's **"Whoa! Wait! WHAAAAAT???!!!"** It seems he's got a "hidden" inner laughter going on.

It's as if Abraham is thinking, *"Unbelievable! Really? Us old people have a child! Ha-ha-ha!!!*

Do you find it odd? Abraham laughed, but I've never heard a sermon on it. Most people only pick on Sarah for laughing. We find her story a bit later in Genesis 18:9-15. God showed up again and pronounced, *"Within a year Sarah will give birth."* She overheard, and laughed.

Read Genesis 18:9-15.

> 9 They said to him, "Where is Sarah your wife?" And he said, "She is in the tent."10 The Lord said, "I will surely return to you about this time next year, and Sarah your wife shall have a son." And Sarah was listening at the tent door behind him.11 Now Abraham and Sarah were old, advanced in years. The way of women had ceased to be with Sarah. 12 So Sarah laughed to herself, saying, "After I am worn out, and my lord is old, shall I have pleasure?" 13 The Lord said to Abraham, "Why did Sarah laugh and

> say, 'Shall I indeed bear a child, now that I am old?' 14 Is anything too hard for the Lord? At the appointed time I will return to you, about this time next year, and Sarah shall have a son." 15 But Sarah denied it, saying, "I did not laugh," for she was afraid. He said, "No, but you did laugh."

God confronted Sarah about her laughter and she denied it. But, He knew her heart, and I believe His reply, *"No, but you did laugh."* is similar to Jesus' encounter with the Samaritan woman at the well. (John 4:16-18) When he asked her to go get her husband, she replied, *"I have no husband."* Jesus then told her, with no condemnation, that she was right, she'd had five husbands and the one she was with was not her husband. Jesus confronted her with grace.

God confronted Sarah's unbelief with grace.

He had made a covenant-promise earlier, and He never goes back on His word. This may have been her first personal encounter with God, and she literally became the mother of laughter. Isaac's name means laughter.

You might say she got what she laughed for!

And so did we! This JOY-loving God – He came down from Heaven to covenant with us, to dwell in us, among us, to lift us, and love us – He delights to be gracious to us. This should fill our hearts to overflow with joy; it should stir us to erupt in laughter at the magnitude of the sheer, unbelievable grace of it!

God's covenant grace covers our faithlessness; He gives us what He's promised, despite us

Digging Deeper

What about you? Do you find yourself right now in the dust? Are you kneeling at Jesus' feet? Do you feel unqualified for what you are being called to do? Are you facing a seemingly insurmountable challenge? Are you waiting on a dream to come to pass? A promise? Are you stuck in something you have no idea how you'll ever get out?

What is it you're currently seeking from God that you are certain aligns with His character and His will? (Maybe you simply long to know His will about something, you can start there.)

Read 2 Corinthians 1:18-22

- **Write the last seven words of verse 19 from the ESV translation.**

- **Where does the YES come from? (Verse 20)**

- **His promises for us are all "Yes" in Him, so we can give a hearty *Amen!* Just to make sure you seal this truth in your heart . . . How many promises can you say Amen to?**

- **What is our Amen ultimately for?**

Stop now, Pray. Ask God for a promise or promises to claim regarding what you are seeking from Him. You might need to do some digging with a concordance, Google, or Biblegateway.com. Write what you find below:

Read the following scriptures:

If you abide in me, and my words abide in you, ask whatever you wish, and it will be done for you. John 15:7

You did not choose me, but I chose you and appointed you that you should go and bear fruit and that your fruit should abide, so that whatever you ask the Father in my name, he may give it to you. John 15:16

Now, ask God to increase your faith. Ask Him to help you remember to pray using the promises He has given to you.

God Has Us

The fact that we who are in Christ, are in a covenant relationship with Him, should sturdy our faith in His promises. We are told His promises are ALL "Yes and Amen" yet we still find ourselves doubting . . . doubting that our prayers are valuable, doubting that they are heard, doubting that the thing we are seeking will ever happen.

We need to remember how the Lord our God CHOSE us to be His, then put His spirit in us to seal His covenant. In so doing, He has secured for us everything we need for doing His will.

He who started a good work in us, WILL be faithful to complete it.
(Philippians 1:6)

Both our human nature and the enemy of our souls will work against our faith if we let them. It is by grabbing hold of the absolute assurance of the faithfulness of God to do what He has promised, that we move forward by faith, praying fervently for His will to be done on earth as it is in Heaven.

So, if you find yourself falling on your knees in the dust at His feet, or flat out on the carpet in laughter, you can be assured He is delighted to have you approach Him in humble faith, and He will fulfill His every purpose for you.

Our God is a covenant keeper. With Him there is no shifting! He will perfect that which concerns you. He will keep you blameless, in Him, for the great day of our triumphal wedding feast in Heaven.

Believe in His Promises.

Fall on your face in the overwhelming place.

Wait faithfully for His timing.

Prayer Prompt

Based on the promise in John 15:16, pen a prayer to God. Include in your prayer any promises God has given you for what you are waiting on Him for.

You did not choose me, but I chose you and appointed you that you should go and bear fruit and that your fruit should abide, so that whatever you ask the Father in my name, he may give it to you. John 15:16

And Jacob was left alone. And a man wrestled with him until the breaking of the day. When the man saw that he did not prevail against Jacob, he touched his hip socket, and Jacob's hip was put out of joint as he wrestled with him.
Genesis 32:24-25

"The degree of blessing enjoyed by any man will correspond exactly with the completeness of God's victory over him."
"God conquered Jacob by weakening him." [1]
Warren Wiersbe

1

How Does God Remake Us?

Just as stories in the Bible display God's work in the lives of His people, as believers our lives are also stories seen by the people around us.

We should steward our stories for the glory of God. As we map out our experiences, remembering significant moments, and processing them with the Holy Spirit, we will see that our relationships (or lack thereof) with our parents play a significant role. Parental ties are ordained by God to shape us for His purposes.

Tracing God's hand in Jacob's story will encourage us as daughters of God, and as parents if we've been gifted with children, that His grace is always working toward His will being accomplished.

Observing family interactions in scripture can teach us about human nature. We learn of God's grace for our failures and see His abundant goodness poured out despite the fact that we don't deserve it.

As we walk through Jacob's story, be mindful of your own. Be listening for the Holy Spirit to show you highlights from your life that He wants to deal with or those that He already has dealt with. Then you will be able to tell of God's wonderful works to those around you and to the next generation.

I Am Weak

Unreasonable fears marked my childhood. If I were to name them, the primary two would be "Fear of Rejection" and "Fear of Authority" – I especially feared making my dad angry.

It seemed that rejection was a continual part of my life, and I just dealt with its daggers as they pierced, often telling people what I thought -- *in my mind* -- but never, ever with my lips.

Somehow, my method of inner self-justification pacified the often-felt sting to my heart. But, it left me with a lot of baggage as an adult.

I enjoyed a reprieve from painful feelings of rejection by my peers during the school day after stepping off of the bus. Although I was accepted and loved at home, even there, I spent much effort on avoiding disappointing my dad.

Part of my fear stemmed from watching him be angry with others. Like so many people, in impatient moments, he'd utter words of disapproval. When he would rebuke my little sister, my heart hurt. My empathy caused me to wince as if I were the one being rebuked. I was *hypersensitive*.

Dad often told his friends, *"I never have to spank Bean; she'll start to cry if I even look like I might."*

Though you can sense his fondness for me by the use of the nickname, and I knew he loved me beyond a shadow of a doubt, I still feared his disapproval.

Over the years, I learned to "read" my dad in order to please him. I liked to feel his favor. I might have even believed I was his favorite. Seeking that position caused me to give up many things as a child. I'd prefer to work for my dad, because it made him happy. When Dad was happy, I was happy.

However, being so involved in working for my dad kept me from having a life outside of my occupation as a 'farmer's daughter'. This only fueled the feelings of rejection I endured while I was at school. I sought to improve myself in order to be loved and accepted. I often studied the popular girls to try to figure out their secret.

Striving marked my growing up years. I learned the art of self-preservation and was labeled by a word that often describes firstborns, *"responsible."*

When I first began my relationship with Jesus, I understood and received His grace, but I still struggled with condemnation when I'd sin. About ten years in, during a very stressful season, I felt rejected by Him. Rather than trusting in His love, I began to strive to please Him just as I had in my childhood with my earthly father.

Because I was trying to please God in my own strength, I ended up in a deep pit of anxiety and depression. As the word "pit" suggests, it was a scary, dark place. And I wasn't the only one who was afraid of it. The closest people in my life were scared too. They understandably wanted me to just get over what I was going through. But the pressure I felt to get better actually made things worse.

It was as if shame and condemnation had a noose around my neck. I was overtaken by my greatest fears. I felt rejected and alone; I could barely breathe.

It took several years of relentlessly pursuing God for my healing. I eventually found rest and joy in Jesus' love. Through renewing my mind in His word, having a mentor pray with me weekly, and holding on for dear life to God's promises, I was lifted out of the pit.

Looking back, it's as if the Lord gave me over to what I was prone to rely on (myself) in order for me to experience His unconditional love and power. Only He could deliver me from the lies that strangled me. Just as we will read in the story of Jacob's life, God knew exactly what I needed to overcome what bound me.

Several years later, I was walking with a friend as she sought Jesus to deliver her out of her own pit. One day after meeting with her, I got in my car and, with astonishment, tears of thanksgiving spilled over as I told the Lord, *"Thank you that I went through that!"* Because I knew my experience had enabled me to effectively minister to her as she gained victory over the darkness.

God Remakes

Abraham and Sarah gave birth to their promised son, Isaac. Isaac took a wife named Rebekah, and after Isaac prayed for her womb to be opened, Rebekah got pregnant with twins.

Rebekah felt the babies struggling within her, and asked God, *"Why is this happening to me?"*

God graciously replied to her question, *"Two nations are in your womb, and two peoples from within you shall be divided; the one shall be stronger than the other, the older shall serve the younger." (Genesis 25:23)*

God answered Isaac's prayer by opening Rebekah's womb, and He answered her question about her boys. Let's consider the reason that prayer is mentioned or conversations are recorded for us in scripture.

Why do we have an account of Isaac's prayer for God to open the womb? Why would God even tell Rebekah about her boys and His purposes for them? Certainly He knew that she would use her own methods to obtain the prophesied outcome. Could it be that any true conversation with God results in momentum? Might our prayers be His way of moving His will forward in the earth? At the very least, the recorded conversations display relationships.

Let a holy hush fall upon your heart at the significance of your own relationship with the God of the universe. He wants to advance His Kingdom mission through you in a unique way.You, displaying His glory. Marvel at the fact that His work often hinges on your prayers and conversations with Him. God is less concerned about our perfection and more focused on us, living in communion with Him.

Jacob, the second born, came out of his mother grasping the heel of his firstborn brother, Esau.

Jacob's name means, "heel grabber" or "he cheats."

> When the boys grew up, Esau was a skillful hunter, a man of the field, while Jacob was a quiet man, dwelling in tents. Isaac loved Esau because he ate of his game, but Rebekah loved Jacob.
> Genesis 25:27-28

Each parent had a favorite. It's hard not to pause and laugh at the reason Isaac favored Esau. This preference for hearty food reminds us of a modern cliché regarding the road to a man's heart (. . . is through his stomach). This idea may have its foundation all the way back here in this Genesis story, rather than what we might assume to be in a 1950's American kitchen.

Isaac loved his boy because he brought home tasty meat to eat.

It's hard to know for sure if Rebekah favored Jacob because she was overcompensating for Isaac's obvious favoring of his "manly son" or if her favor was due to the fact that Jacob closely reflected her own disposition. As a female, it's not hard to imagine both being true.

Jacob's first recorded trick was to meet his brother coming home from a hunt -- hungry, with a pot of stew. Esau approached him for a bowl, and Jacob offered a trade.

Esau, being overdramatic, and thinking only of the present moment, replied, *"I am about to die; of what use is a birthright to me?"*

In one hungry moment, he despised his birthright by trading it for a bowl of stew.

The next time we encounter Jacob, the cheater, is when his father is old, his eyes nearly blind. In preparation for his death, Isaac called Esau and told him to go hunt game and make him a delicious meal so he could deliver the blessing on his firstborn son before he dies.

As Rebekah heard the exchange, wanting Jacob to receive Esau's blessing, she began a deceptive plot of her own. She instigated her plan by helping make delicious food and then disguising Jacob so he smells and feels like Esau.

Wearing Esau's clothing to emulate the fragrance of the hunter, complete with hairy goatskins fastened to his arms to mimic Esau's, Jacob brings the delicious food to Isaac.

Oh, the power of stew!

This part of the story highlights our human weakness and tendency to fixate on temporal things. We often fail to look beyond our immediate needs. When we rely on ourselves and hold too tightly to things of this world, we will experience significant spiritual loss.

Notice an absence of any conversation with God in these verses.

Their deceptive plan works, and Isaac pours forth the blessing for the firstborn onto his second born son, Jacob.

Shortly after Jacob left the tent, Esau entered the scene, food in hand, anticipating his blessing. He and his father suddenly became aware they've been duped. Esau pleaded for another blessing, but there was not one to be given.

Esau, twice tricked, now hates Jacob and wants to kill him.

Rebekah "comes to the rescue" *again*, intending to guard her beloved Jacob, and she urges him to go to her homeland. She convinces Isaac to send him away with a blessing, to marry and be fruitful, which he does.

Jacob leaves home. On the way to Haran, he stops for the night, and finds a stone to use for a pillow. As he sleeps, he has a dream.

Read Genesis 28:12-21

> 12 And he dreamed, and behold, there was a ladder set up on the earth, and the top of it reached to heaven. And behold, the angels of God were ascending and descending on it! 13 And behold, the Lord stood above it and said, "I am the Lord, the God of Abraham your father and the God of Isaac. The land on which you lie I will give to you and to your offspring. 14 Your offspring shall be like the dust of the earth, and you shall spread abroad to the west and to the east and to the north and to the south, and in you and your offspring shall all the families of the earth be blessed. 15 Behold, I am with you and will keep you wherever you go, and will bring you back to this land. For I will not leave you until I have done what I have promised you." 16 Then Jacob awoke from his sleep and said, "Surely the Lord is in this place, and I did not know it." 17 And he was afraid and said, "How awesome is this place! This is none other than the house of God, and this is the gate of heaven."
>
> 18 So early in the morning Jacob took the stone that he had put under his head and set it up for a pillar and poured oil on the top of it. 19 He called the name of that place Bethel, but the name of the city was Luz at the first. 20 Then Jacob made a vow, saying, "If God will be with me and will keep me in this way that I go, and will give me bread to eat and clothing to wear, 21 so that I come again to my father's house in peace, then the Lord shall be my God ...

Jacob is headed into a wilderness where he will experience the ramifications of his own methods. On his way, God meets him at Bethel and promises him the land he is lying on and that he will multiply greatly. He also promises to be with him, watch over him, bless him and bring him back to this land.

This meeting with God, and the promises God speaks over Jacob are significant. It's likely they echoed in his heart throughout his wilderness years. This is significant for us too, because God has written promises over each one of us to sustain us in our wilderness times.

Jacob comes to his uncle Laban's house and falls in love with his beautiful daughter, Rachel. Laban, seeing the desire in his nephew, takes advantage of his hunger, and tricks him into working for him fourteen years without pay.

During those years, God humbled Jacob, who began to trust God. Eventually, in a battle of wits with his uncle, God turns the tables again -- on Laban -- and prospers Jacob with both children and livestock.

When the time comes for him to return to his parents and face Esau, God blesses Jacob. He finally leaves Haran as a wealthy man, with all of his people and flocks and herds. As he moves toward his homeland, with more than a little fear and trepidation, he is literally facing his past.

During the wilderness years, Jacob's heart was softened.

During our wilderness years,

our hearts are softened.

In God's grace and wisdom, our wilderness seasons are designed for our refining. Jacob's story can encourage us to trust God in difficult times, and believe that He will perfect that which concerns us! (See Psalm 138:8 KJV) We have assurance of victory over our old ways!

Along the way home, Jacob finds himself returning to the site of his dream where God meets with him again.

Read Genesis 32:22-31

> 22 The same night he arose and took his two wives, his two female servants, and his eleven children, and crossed the ford of the Jabbok. 23 He took them and sent them across the stream, and everything else that he had. 24 And Jacob was left alone. And a man wrestled with him until the breaking of the day. 25 When the man saw that he did not prevail against Jacob, he touched his hip socket, and Jacob's hip was put out of joint as he wrestled with him. 26 Then he said, "Let me go, for the day has broken." But Jacob said, "I will not let you go unless you bless me."27 And he said to him, "What is your name?" And he said, "Jacob." 28 Then he said, "Your name shall no longer be called Jacob, but Israel, for you have striven with God and with men, and have prevailed." 29 Then Jacob asked him, "Please tell me your name." But he said, "Why is it that you ask my name?" And there he blessed him. 30 So Jacob called the name of the place Peniel, saying, "For I have seen God face to face, and yet my life has been delivered." 31 The sun rose upon him as he passed Penuel, limping because of his hip.

Jacob wrestles with the angel of God until sunrise. The entire scene speaks of Jacob's relentless pursuit to cling to God. This proves that he is a changed man. And he leaves God's presence, physically changed.

God will give us reminders of His work in our lives to prevent us from relapsing into our old ways.

You might recall from **Genesis 28:20-21,** Jacob's words:

> Then Jacob made a vow, saying, "If God will be with me and will keep me in this way that I go, and will give me bread to eat and clothing to wear, so that I come again to my father's house in peace, then the Lord shall be my God, and this stone which I have set up for a pillar shall be God's house.

Jacob went hoping to find God, and God intended to show Himself to Jacob.

God asks Jacob his name. Not because He didn't know it, but to give Jacob opportunity to own up to it, as if he was confessing, "I am a cheater."

Upon his confession, God changes his name to Israel. Israel means "he struggled with God" Jacob struggled all night to hang on, or to cling to God, and he left God's presence changed. His life was forever knit to God.

Digging Deeper

Read Matthew 16:13-19

- **Write the question Jesus asked in verse 13:**

- **What answers were given to Jesus in verse 14?**

- **Write out Peter's response to Jesus question (verse 16):**

- **In three words, how does Jesus begin to address Simon Bar-Jonah (Peter, son of John, in verse 17)?**

Look up Genesis 32:26.

- **Write out Jacob's reply to the Lord's words, *"Let me go, for the day has broken."***

Look again at Matthew 16:17-18, Jesus suddenly calls Simon Bar-Jonah by another name. Write it here:

- **Who revealed the truth of who Jesus is to Simon Bar-Jonah?**

Jesus speaks a prophetic word over Peter in verse 18: "You are Peter, and on this rock I will build my church, and the gates of hell shall not prevail against it.

- **What do you think Jesus is referring to when He says, "on this rock"? Do you think He is building His church on Peter? Or do you think He is building His church on this rock-solid revelation that God the Father just gave to Peter?**

- **Have you had a prophetic word spoken over you by someone? (Or a word directly from the Father about you?) Write it down and talk to God about it. Use the lined page at the end of this chapter, or your study journal to record in.**

- **Journal about your walk with God so far. What kinds of things did you do before you met him to find love? Are you still primarily using those methods or do you periodically fall into them because the Lord has matured you? What are some promises the Lord has spoken over your life?**

God With Us

When we meet Jesus, we are given a new identity as *blessed* daughters of God, but we are not instantly transformed into His image. We enter into a process called sanctification, whereby we are gradually transformed from "glory to glory" -- we continually become more like Him as He refines us to reflect Him to the world. When we get to Heaven, we will be completely like Him for we shall see Him as He is.

Until then, we will have a wilderness season or seasons, where we discover who God is by experiencing His love and power in our lives. During these refining seasons, we will also discover the inadequacy of our own ways. He lovingly brings us through the wilderness to a place of humble surrender and trust.

There comes a time when we come full circle, where we will wrestle to hold on to the promises He has spoken over our lives. In our wrestling, we become the people He intends for us to be, bearing rich fruit for the Kingdom of God.

It seems the re-naming in scripture consistently includes a divine revelation of God, and a more unified relationship with God.

We each have wilderness time with God.

God reveals Himself to us uniquely,
and personalizes His revelation.

We must struggle to hold on
to God's promises.

Prayer Prompt

Write a prayer expressing any sorrow, fear, or need that you currently have, and then express your confidence in God's promise to bring you out into a spacious place.

OR, if you are currently not experiencing refining fire in your life, write a prayer of praise and thanksgiving for the work He has done in your life to this point.

And after you have suffered a little while, the God of all grace, who has called you to his eternal glory in Christ, will himself restore, confirm, strengthen, and establish you.
1 Peter 5:10

He brought me out into a broad place; he rescued me, because he delighted in me.
Psalm 18:19

3

HANNAH

fervent & overflowing

She was deeply distressed and prayed to the Lord and wept bitterly. And she vowed a vow and said, "O Lord of hosts, if you will indeed look on the affliction of your servant and remember me and not forget your servant, but will give to your servant a son, then I will give him to the Lord all the days of his life, and no razor shall touch his head."
1 Samuel 1:10-12

You open your hand;
you satisfy the desire of every living thing.
Psalm 145:16

How Does God Satisfy Our Desires?

We are all born with a huge crater, a gaping inner "emotional hole" needing to be filled.

You might say we come out of the womb holding an invisible empty bucket.

This could explain the birth pains . . . *just saying* . . . And actually, multiplied pain in bearing children is one of the consequences of the fall, the curse pronounced by God on daughters of Eve. (Genesis 3:16)

The empty bucket is symbolic of the absence of God in our unregenerate souls.

God means to fill our vacancies with His abundant love and His rich goodness.

The good news, the Gospel, is that Jesus *is* the fulfillment of our every need and longing.

> He who did not spare his own Son but gave him up for us all, how will he not also with him graciously give us all things? Romans 8:32

Imagine yourself as a child, carrying an empty bucket wherever you went. The side of your bucket said, "I want love." How did you try to get it filled? What methods might you still use to earn love?

God has built within us inherent needs. We literally feel these needs and we are meant to have them fulfilled, but not by anyone or anything less than God. This is where idolatry enters our heart. When we seek our fulfillment in the wrong place or through the wrong thing, it is a false god. If we worship people or anything else besides God; this is called "idolatry" in the Bible.

In Bible times, people literally worshipped statues. But what do we worship today? Where do you go to get your bucket filled besides God?

I Ache With Longing

The years I suffered with anxiety and depression come up often in my conversations. I apologize for this, feeling as if I sound like a broken record. It happens to be one of the most significant seasons of my journey because by it, God did a powerful transforming work in my life.

I didn't know that I had lived my life getting my bucket filled by people pleasing. I was unaware that I was chained by my perfectionism. My mind equated my polished performance with being loveable. This created deep fear of failure and deep shame. I had people on pedestals, and I was proverbially laying at their feet.

God humbled me by allowing me to be in a place I could not perform my way out of. When I was stuck and helpless, He proved His unconditional love, mercy, and power as He redeemed my life from the pit. It was His truth that set me free.

I needed to come to understand that I am loved because He IS love. I can't earn love, I can only respond to His. I've learned that I can't even give love unless He pours it into me. Unless it's His pure love, my acts of love have tainted motives.

Praise God He knows how to deliver His children from flawed thinking!

We will be given many opportunities to be tested in what we learn during our wilderness seasons. Lessons learned in the darkest times of our lives often prove to be valuable in the Lord's mission.

The Empty Bucket

Let's look at the God-designed needs of every human soul: [1]

- **Love and Acceptance:** We are meant to be free of shame, fully loved, and experience belonging to a family.

1

- **Significance and Security:** As stewards of God's creation, we are designed to rule or lead. God means for us to be protected within secure boundaries, to have abundant provision, and to exercise authority in overcoming difficulty.

- **Care and Empathy:** We have a need for food, clothing and shelter, both physically and spiritually.God designed us to be fully known, loved and cared for.

- **Creative expression:** As image-bearers of our Creator, we are meant to express ourselves creatively and to reproduce.

- **Rest:** He gave us a desire and need for peace, ease, harmony, and absence of tension.

- **Freedom:** We are created to make choices, have control, and enjoy spontaneity. He built us to delight in decisions and in naming things.

- **Dominion and Leadership:** God has given us a heart for stewardship of our domain. He's given us authority, power and leadership longings. We were meant to subdue and rule in the earth. We are meant to be godly examples worthy of emulation.

- **Justice:** We naturally desire fairness, equal scales, and impartiality. God has no favorites.

- **Worship:** We were created to know mighty God-King, to acknowledge Him as provider and protector and to trust Him with all of our hearts.

Whenever the Lord allows tight places, unfulfilled longings, rejections, loss, or painful transitions, He is testing us to prove Himself and improve us.

God Satisfies

In 1 Samuel 1, we find a story of a man named Elkanah who had two wives. Hannah, and Peninnah. (Let's call her Penny.)

Penny had children.
Hannah had no children.

As we've already seen in our study, children were a woman's glory. To be without children was a sign of inferiority in Biblical culture.

Every year, Elkanah took his family to Shiloh to worship. When he sacrificed to the Lord, he gave portions of the sacrifices to his wives. He gave a double portion to Hannah,

"For he loved her, though the Lord had closed her womb."

And her rival (Penny) used to provoke her grievously to irritate her, because the Lord had closed her womb. (1 Samuel 1:5)

Year after year, Penny continued to antagonize Hannah to the point that Hanna would cry and not even taste of the food her husband had lavished on her. Elkanah couldn't understand how or why his love wasn't enough for Hannah.

One time during their worship, Hannah's pain had reached a pinnacle. She intently set her face to pursue the Lord after the meal, the one she had not eaten. She entered the temple where she prayed fervently to the Lord to grant her a son, promising God that she would dedicate him to the Lord if He would answer her request.

Eli was the priest at the time. Though his character was suffering greatly from apathy and irreverence (1 Samuel 2:29,) he had taken his position in the temple that day. His presence in the Lord's house indicated that he still had at least a small regard for God's law within his heart. From his seat by the doorpost, he saw Hannah mouthing her prayers and assumed that she was drunk. He accused her of such, but she refuted his criticism, explaining her deep longing and the fervency of her prayers.

As God would have it, the one with spiritual authority in the temple that day was Eli. In response to Hannah's prayer of faith, he blessed Hannah, saying,

"Go in peace, and the God of Israel grant your petition that you have made to him."

Hannah believed and received the blessing in the moment of hearing his words, as she replied to Eli,

> "Let your servant find favor in your eyes." Then the woman went her way and ate, and her face was no longer sad. (1 Samuel 1:16-20)

Think about that. Eli told her to *"Go in peace."* And that is exactly what she did!

By faith she believed and received the blessing, as indicated by the sudden shift in her countenance.

Scripture says then, *"in due time, the Lord remembered her prayer, and she conceived."*

When Hannah took her empty bucket to the Lord, He filled it with the sweetest gift-- who grew up to be one of the greatest prophets in the Old Testament. Her boy would be the one to anoint David as Israel's King. David, in turn, would become the forefather of our Heavenly King, Jesus. Talk about overflow!

She who seeks God with her empty bucket will receive a multitude of eternal blessings!

Hannah gave birth to Samuel, and when the time came, she brought him to the Temple, and he was placed under the care of Eli, the anointed one that had spoken the blessing over Hannah. Eli received the honor of investing in her son.

It is evident in the story of Hannah's life, that she was a woman who did not retaliate. She didn't seek to fill her deep void through some other means, as Sarai, Abram's wife, had done.

Read Genesis 16:1-5

> 16 Now Sarai, Abram's wife, had borne him no children. She had a female Egyptian servant whose name was Hagar. 2 And Sarai said to Abram, "Behold now, the Lord has prevented me from bearing children. Go in to my servant; it may be that I shall obtain children by her." And Abram listened to the voice of Sarai.3 So, after Abram had lived ten years in the land of Canaan, Sarai, Abram's wife, took Hagar the Egyptian, her servant, and gave her to Abram her husband as a wife. 4 And he went in to Hagar, and she conceived. And when she saw that she had conceived, she looked with contempt on her mistress. 5 And Sarai said to Abram, "May the wrong done to me be on you! I gave my servant to your embrace, and when she saw that she had conceived, she looked on me with contempt. May the Lord judge between you and me!"

Read Genesis 21:9-10

> But Sarah saw the son of Hagar the Egyptian, whom she had borne to Abraham, laughing. 10 So she said to Abraham, "Cast out this slave woman with her son, for the son of this slave woman shall not be heir with my son Isaac."

What Sarai received when she took matters into her own hands, was conflict.

Sarai and Hagar experienced conflict.
Sarai and Abram experienced conflict.
Ishmael and Isaac experienced conflict.

> For the one who sows to his own flesh will from the flesh reap corruption, but the one who sows to the Spirit will from the Spirit reap eternal life. Galatians 6:8

Hannah exhibited endurance and longsuffering, with her heart perpetually turned toward the Lord. She appears to have understood the fact that if there was a void in her life, it was God alone who could fill it.

She didn't try to win Penny over.
She didn't retaliate, zinging her own word-bombs at her.
She didn't settle for a husband who deeply loved and favored her.

She pressed in to apprehend the desire of her soul, and because of her faith, she received what her heart truly longed for.

> Delight yourself in the Lord and He will give you the desires of your heart. (Psalm 37:4)

Do you trust the Lord for your deepest longings to be fulfilled? Are you pressing into Him and praying, or are you striving by human power to access what only God can give you?

Do you remember what happened in the situation with Sarai offering her maidservant, Hagar to her husband Abraham? Ishmael entered the picture. Just as Penny antagonized Hannah, Ishmael antagonized Isaac, the child of the promise. God spoke over Ishmael, that he would be a wild donkey of a man whose hand would be against everyone.

Our acts done in our own power produce strife and conflict.

Our reliance on the promises of God, and our prayerful pursuit of Him for our deepest longings, brings peace and life.

The choice we each have to make is where we take our empty bucket.

Penny, even though she was given children, acted superior to Hannah. She enjoyed gloating in God's gracious gift. Her womb had been opened, but her bucket remained empty.

"Bareness is the soil in which God grows desperation and a sense of need."
~Eric Ludy [online sermon][2]

God will allow our emptiness only because He intends to fill us with something greater than the things we want. He wants to fill us with nothing less than His Holy Spirit.

2

Digging Deeper

Read Luke 11:5-13

- What is the primary message Jesus relays to the disciples who've asked Him to teach them how to pray?

- What are the three words in verse 9 that Jesus used synonymously with prayer?

- What does Jesus promise in verse 10 to those who pray?

- Does his promise in verse 10 eliminate anyone?

Read verses 11-13 again, and fill in the blank for verse 13, using <u>all caps</u> for the second blank:

If you who are ____________, know how to give good gifts to your children, how much ___________ will the heavenly Father give the _________ ________________ to those who ____________ Him?

- Spend some time thinking about this . . . Could there be a greater gift than that?

Take a look at Ephesians 3:14-19 and highlight all forms of the word "strength."

> 14 … I (Paul) bow my knees before the Father, 15 from whom every family in heaven and on earth is named, 16 that according to the riches of his glory he may grant you to be strengthened with power through his Spirit in your inner being, 17 so that Christ may dwell in your hearts through faith—that you, being rooted and grounded in love, 18 may have strength to comprehend with all the saints what is the breadth and length and height and depth, 19 and to know the love of Christ that surpasses knowledge, that you may be filled with all the fullness of God.

- **What does the power of the Holy Spirit strengthen us to do?**

- **Have you ever considered this to be a need?**

- **Are you strong in comprehending the love of God for YOU?**

- **On a scale of 1-10, how full is your bucket on an average day?**

Now read Ephesians 3:20. Highlight the word in this verse -- the one that you wrote in all caps above -- and underline the word that follows it.

> Now to him who is able to do far more abundantly than all that we ask or think, according to the power at work within us . . .(From Ephesians 3:20)

Read Isaiah 51:1-3 below.

- **Underline every action God wants you to take.**
- **Put a heart around the word "YOU"** *(using a pink or red colored pencil is nice)*
- **Highlight or circle everything the Lord says He will do for you when you do what He calls you to:**

"Listen to me, you who pursue righteousness,

you who seek the Lord:

look to the rock from which you were hewn,

and to the quarry from which you were dug.

Look to Abraham your father

and to Sarah who bore you;

for he was but one when I called him,

that I might bless him and multiply him.

For the Lord comforts Zion;

he comforts all her waste places

and makes her wilderness like Eden,

her desert like the garden of the Lord;

joy and gladness will be found in her,

thanksgiving and the voice of song.

What "MORE" would you like God to do for you? What is your empty bucket? Write a prayer to God based on the deep longing of your heart. And ask someone else to join you in praying for your bucket to be filled with God's overflowing love.

God In Us

Imagine putting all the fire of a star into a galvanized bucket. A star is so hot, the bucket would disintegrate before your eyes. It is no different with the filling of your heart with the very life of God.

It is the Holy Spirit Himself that enables our hearts to contain such fiery love as our Lord has for us! I like to think He is eternal gold that overlays our weak flesh.

When the Spirit strengthens us in our inner being – *our bucket* – He enables and empowers us to receive the immeasurable love of God into our thirsty hearts. Marvel at the miracle! The Star of Bethlehem shines in each of us while we journey in this wilderness, bearing His love-gift on earth.

In all of our dark places, our Heavenly Father wants to say, "Let there be Light!" And when He speaks a word, watch out world!

Our King has all the resources we will ever need. He invites us to come to Him and be filled with His presence. Through our union with Him, our lives are magnificently precious and eternally significant. When we are united with Him, we will bear much spiritual fruit in the land of the living and in the life to come!

This sisters, is the answer to the statement Jesus made. "How much MORE!!!"

We can be like Hannah, and endure hardship like good soldiers.

We can bring our empty bucket to the throne room of God and He will overflow it.

Our words of blessing over others impacts eternity.

Prayer Prompt

Based on Psalm 37:4 and Luke 11:9-10,13 pen a prayer, delighting in and expressing trust to your Heavenly Father to meet your needs and fulfill your dreams.

Delight yourself in the Lord and He will give you the desires of your heart.
Psalm 37:4

And I tell you, ask, and it will be given to you; seek, and you will find; knock, and it will be opened to you. For everyone who asks receives, and the one who seeks finds, and to the one who knocks it will be opened. Luke 11:9-10

If you then, who are evil, know how to give good gifts to your children, how much more will the heavenly Father give the Holy Spirit to those who ask him!"
Luke 11:13

4

JONAH

surrender & salvation

And he said to them, "I am a Hebrew, and I fear the Lord, the God of heaven, who made the sea and the dry land." Then the men were exceedingly afraid and said to him, "What is this that you have done!" For the men knew that he was fleeing from the presence of the Lord, because he had told them.

Therefore they called out to the Lord, "O Lord, let us not perish for this man's life, and lay not on us innocent blood, for you, O Lord, have done as it pleased you."
Jonah 1:9-10

How Does God Move Us In The Right Direction?

You might remember the children's song, *"If you want to be great in God's Kingdom, you must be a servant of all . . . "*

Maybe you've heard it said, "The Kingdom of God is an upside down Kingdom." Jesus tells us that if we love our lives we will lose them, but if we lose our lives, we will save them. The King of Kings and Lord of Lords told us that He didn't come to be served, but to serve and give His life as a ransom for many.

When Adam and Eve chose to disobey God, His Kingdom order was turned upside down. Jesus came to set things right. It's good to remember that His ways are not our own when we face times of suffering or when we face situations we are too afraid to enter into. Whether we are facing crisis, or a calling that makes us shaky, we are being presented a choice... to trust and obey, banking on God's goodness, or to fear and flee assuming His absence.

Obedience and surrender are synonymous for us who walk with God.

Surrender in suffering

is an agent of salvation.

This Was Not My Plan

Still so tiny . . . he was born three and a half weeks early. At six weeks old, he was not yet eight pounds. I kept pushing down a nagging fear about his size, attributing it to his traumatic early birth, which included stopping my labor, followed by an ambulance ride to a better-equipped hospital.

Once we made it to the hospital, it was determined that his lungs were fully developed and I could go ahead and deliver him. After twenty-four painful-fearful hours, the stopping and then re-starting of labor, I'd given birth to our little 5-lb.13-oz. boy.

Projectile vomiting started on a Tuesday of his sixth week. It reeked of rotten eggs. By Friday, he wasn't getting better. Fear, coupled with wisdom, dictated a visit to the Doctor.

We were sent home with instructions to return the next day if things weren't better because of the danger of dehydration. We rallied our troops to pray for our little boy.

Saturday we returned, an x-ray was taken, and we found out Ethan needed surgery. This time we drove ourselves the sixty miles to the better-equipped hospital. Upon arrival, the first order was to get an IV into his veins for fluid.

The kind nurses wanted to save me the trauma of seeing them poke a needle in my baby's head, (the vein in the head is the easier vein to tap into on a little one) so they sought to connect to a vein in his hand . . . and then his other hand . . . and then his feet . . . After trying unsuccessfully five times, they could see my weariness. One of them suggested, *"There is a parent lounge just down the hall, you can go there while we do this."*

I may have been four steps away from his room when I heard his voice crying and I ran back to him. *Dear Lord, please save my boy!*

After seven failed attempts, there was no avoiding putting the needle into the top of his head. By that time, I didn't even care where they put it; I just wanted my baby saved!

When they finally left me alone in the room with Ethan, I bent over his little bassinet and whispered, *"I'm so sorry you've had to go through all this pain. Mommy would never let you suffer unless it was going to save your life. It's just like when Jesus suffered to save us. God the Father had to let His only Son suffer so that we might live. I need to let you suffer for a little while -- so your life can be saved."*

I was certain that the gospel had penetrated his little heart at the sound of my voice, and I was filled with blessed assurance that my baby was going to live.

The next day, Jesus kept me confident as I handed my tiny boy to the surgeon, who scooped him up in his arms and disappeared behind closed doors.

After waiting a little longer than two hours, the surgeon reemerged to tell me that surgery went well and my little man would be fine.

They had to wound his little body so he could have life; an echo of Jesus' love for His Beloved.

Ethan sprouted after that -- everyone said he was making up for lost time. He is all of six foot, four now -- a thriving husband and father who loves the Lord.

God Redirects

Jonah was a prophet to Israel. He was called by God to leave his comfortable home-station, go to the land of their evil enemy and "Call out against it."

God wanted Jonah to warn Nineveh that He was going to judge them.

Read Jonah 1:1-12

> 1 Now the word of the Lord came to Jonah the son of Amittai, saying, 2 "Arise, go to Nineveh, that great city, and call out against it, for their evil has come up before me." 3 But Jonah rose to flee to Tarshish from the presence of the Lord. He went down to Joppa and found a ship going to Tarshish. So he paid the fare and went down into it, to go with them to Tarshish, away from the presence of the Lord.
>
> 4 But the Lord hurled a great wind upon the sea, and there was a mighty tempest on the sea, so that the ship threatened to break up. 5 Then the mariners were afraid, and each cried out to his god. And they hurled the cargo that was in the ship into the sea to lighten it for them. But Jonah had gone down into the inner part of the ship and had lain down and was fast asleep. 6 So the captain came and said to him, "What do you mean, you sleeper? Arise,

> call out to your god! Perhaps the god will give a thought to us, that we may not perish."
>
> 10 Then the men were exceedingly afraid and said to him, "What is this that you have done!" For the men knew that he was fleeing from the presence of the Lord, because he had told them.
>
> 11 Then they said to him, "What shall we do to you, that the sea may quiet down for us?" For the sea grew more and more tempestuous. 12 He said to them, "Pick me up and hurl me into the sea; then the sea will quiet down for you, for I know it is because of me that this great tempest has come upon you."

Interestingly, we find a form of the word "hurl" no less than four times in the first chapter of Jonah. It is used once in regard to God's "gift" of violent wind, and the other three times describing aggressively throwing things (or a man) overboard into the sea. If you would read of Nineveh's barbaric activities, the horrific things they did to their enemies, your stomach might want to hurl its own cargo. To spare you, let's just say, it was worse than we might imagine a Halloween horror movie to be.

Jonah . . . you might know the story . . . he tucked tail and ran the opposite direction of Nineveh. He sought to run away from God' presence. We might assume that many in Israel believed God's presence to be contained only inside the Temple because clearly, Jonah didn't understand the omnipresence of God.

Remember David's words in Psalm 139:7-12?

Where shall I go from your Spirit?
Or where shall I flee from your presence?
If I ascend to heaven, you are there!
If I make my bed in Sheol, you are there!
If I take the wings of the morning
and dwell in the uttermost parts of the sea,
even there your hand shall lead me,
and your right hand shall hold me.
If I say, "Surely the darkness shall cover me,
and the light about me be night,"
even the darkness is not dark to you;
the night is bright as the day,
for darkness is as light with you.

Jonah purchased a ticket and set sail toward Tarshish. But the Lord was in hot pursuit.

> But the Lord hurled a great wind upon the sea, and there was a mighty tempest on the sea, so that the ship threatened to break up. Jonah 1:4

The mariners feared. Each of them cried out to their god, and hurled their cargo into the sea, seeking to lighten the load.

Where is Jonah?
Sleeping.
During a storm.
Who can sleep during a storm?!!

Seeing the failure of their efforts in calming the storm, the Captain seems to have gone looking for some other answer. When he found Jonah sleeping, he was as astonished as we might be.

> "What do you mean, you sleeper? Arise, call out to your god! Perhaps the god will give a thought to us, that we may not perish." Jonah 1:6

Evidently Jonah was silent at first. So the men, desperate for an answer and believing the gods would tell them who was responsible for the storm; in their continued fervor to save their lives, they "cast lots" (their version of drawing straws.)

God Himself pointed "the straw" at Jonah!

> The lot is cast into the lap, but its every decision is from the LORD. (Proverbs 16:33)

Suddenly Jonah couldn't avoid the truth. He had a decision to make.

Having already told them he was running from God, Jonah decided to reveal the identity of the God he was fleeing, *"I am a Hebrew who fears the God of Heaven, who made the sea and dry land."*

Already full of fear, the men became *exceedingly afraid*, and were also astonished at his foolishness. The pagan men's fear of God seemed to be greater than the prophet who served Him!

They asked him, *"What shall we do to you, that the sea may quiet down for us?"*

Jonah answers *"Pick me up and hurl me into the sea. This is all my fault."*

The other sailors are reluctant to do so, clearly afraid of Jonah's God. So they did what we often do in a storm, they set out to row more vigorously. But, in short order, they found themselves no match for God. They decide to entertain Jonah's suggestion. Much to their credit, they PRAY, crying out to Jonah's God! They seek His pardon for throwing His man into the sea, and tell him their fear of being found guilty of shedding innocent blood.

We might surmise that the God of Israel was famous with these mariners.

Maybe they'd heard stories of His power and might, which served them as a foundation for faith in the moment of their very up-close and personal encounter with Him.

Let's pause here and consider the potential rich fruit of our lips when we offer praise to His name. When we tell of His mighty deeds, and thank Him for His goodness in our lives, what might the results be?

> And you will say in that day: "Give thanks to the LORD, call upon his name, make known his deeds among the peoples, proclaim that his name is exalted. (Isaiah 12:4)

Essentially, Jonah's confession and willingness to die in order for his shipmates to live was not only an act of repentance on Jonah's part, but also radical intercession.

Intercession: The English word is derived from Latin intercedo, "to come between" which strangely has the somewhat opposed meanings of "obstruct" and "to interpose on behalf of" a person, and finally "to intercede" .

Jonah's disobedience had put the mariners' lives in danger. His confession and the offering of his life thrust himself between the men and their looming death.

After God ceased the raging sea, we read in Jonah 1:16, "Then the men feared the Lord exceedingly, and they offered a sacrifice to the Lord and made vows."

Instead of fearing the storm,

fear the God of the storm.

This is an oft-overlooked part of Jonah's story. Usually we focus on Jonah's disobedience, on his repentance and deliverance from the belly of the whale. We remember his repentance and salvation of the Ninevites.

These are certainly the emphasis of his story, but pausing to focus on the prayer of those pagan mariners whose lives were in danger, and the willingness of Jonah to offer his life for their safety, gives us a brilliant picture of the power of God at work. As we surrender our lives to the Lord and take up the call to intercede for God's mission on the earth for Heaven, we get to participate in redemption!

The incredible grace hidden in this story can be found in seeing the way that God will allow even our detours to serve His purposes of salvation.

Digging Deeper

Look up and read Matthew 8:23-27

- **What are the similarities to Jonah's story in chapter one?**

- **What are the differences?**

Jonah repented, and underwent a baptism. Those whose lives were in danger because of his disobedience, were saved because he repented.

- **Who might be saved because you turned to Jesus? (Just think of it!)**

- **Jonah's song in chapter two resembles what we understand of the death, burial and resurrection of our King, Jesus. Look up Jonah 2:1-10 and write out the last five words of verse 9:**

Read Romans 6:3 and think about similarities in your own story and Jonah's. When you ran, did God lovingly give you a storm? Did He break the road you were on?

- **Keeping Jonah's song in mind, write out your own praise song to your Savior:**

- **Prayerfully read 1 Timothy 2:1 and respond to the way the Lord speaks.** (We will unpack more about intercession in the next chapter.)

The Jews believed that the seas were reservoirs of evil forces, so even though the disciples had seen Jesus do mighty miracles already, knowing this sheds light on what might seem to be unreasonable fear of the waters. Jesus displayed His power over the waters on numerous occasions.

We could wonder if the disciples were thinking of the story of Jonah when this was happening and Jesus was sleeping. Perhaps they wondered, "who sinned?" and what was to become of them – who would need to be hurled out to sea?

Look up Hebrews 7:25

- **Who is able to save to the uttermost?**

- **What does He constantly live to do?**

- **Will He ever fail?**

God Owns Us

When we belong to God and are filled with His Spirit, we find He brings us to many "altars." We must entrust to Him our sick child, our broken finances, our reputation, our safety, our homes, our possessions, and our painful relationships. Whatever He calls us to do or endure or surrender, we can know that He will bring resurrection life from it.

Our surrender and obedience bears fruit for the Kingdom of God. Every time. As a result of our letting go, eternal treasures are being stored up for us!

Jonah was a prophet of God; the Spirit of God was upon him wherever he went. Since we are born of the Spirit, the same is true of us, but more because He lives in us. As "Temples," we are filled with God and God surrounds us. Think of the places you've been recently, and consider the people who have had an opportunity to encounter God simply because you are His daughter. How might you pray for or serve those people?

Intercession is costly. Thankfully, Jesus has paid the ultimate price. All we need to do is surrender to Him; our lives are eternally safe! He is in our boat, and we need not jump ship!

How is God asking you to trust and obey and pray today?

Our detours will be used to bring salvation when we surrender them.

Never underestimate the power of testifying about God's goodness to you.

Jesus is the great Redeemer;
He is mighty to save.

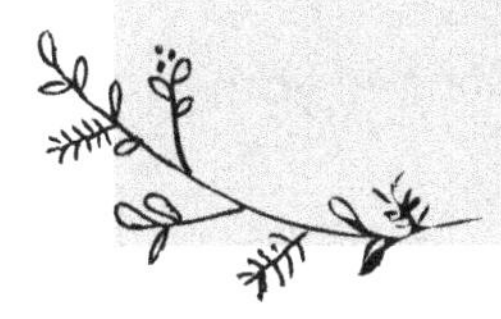

Prayer Prompt

As you meditate on Isaiah 41:18 and Jonah 2:9, listen for the Lord's voice to you personally. Often in our darkest places, His voice comes through a whisper. Ask Him to speak, and then write down what you hear. Close your prayer with praise and thanksgiving.

I will open rivers on the bare heights, and fountains in the midst of the valleys. I will make the wilderness a pool of water, and the dry land springs of water. Isaiah 41:18

But I with the voice of thanksgiving will sacrifice to you; what I have vowed I will pay.
Salvation belongs to the LORD!" Jonah 2:9

5

MOSES

intercedes & advances

And the Lord said to Moses, "Go down, for your people, whom you brought up out of the land of Egypt, have corrupted themselves . . .
Now therefore let me alone, that my wrath may burn hot against them and I may consume them, in order that I may make a great nation of you.
Exodus 32:7,10

But Moses implored the Lord his God and said, "O Lord, why does your wrath burn hot against your people, whom you have brought out of the land of Egypt with great power and with a mighty hand?
Exodus 32:11

How Do I Get Close To God?

If you do a Google search on *bonding* or *steps to build relationships*, you'll find the top results will have to do with conversation. As you seek to build bonds with others, topping the list of suggestions will be *ask questions* or instigate fun dialogue, such as:

For couples:
1. Ask, "How was your day, Hon?" 2. Laugh over inside jokes.
For friends:
1. Ask about family, friends, and pets. 2. Ask about interests, hobbies and thoughts on current events.

Emotional bonds result from time spent together and having shared experiences. With friends, sometimes these bind us together for life, and other times, we move away for a myriad of reasons. Friendships are non-contractual. You may have heard it said, *"You can choose your friends, but you're stuck with your family."*

Familial bonds are unbreakable. Those who came through the same womb and/or were fathered by the same seed-sower, are bonded for life by their bloodlines.

Since we are sinful people living in a sinful world, our commitments too often shatter. As a result of the brokenness we experience, we might fail to believe God's dedication to fulfill every promise He has made to us. When we find ourselves in painful circumstances, we often doubt He is actually working it all for our good and for His good purposes.

It will benefit us to grapple with our struggle with unbelief regarding God's unconditional love due to the fact that people have failed us. He wants us to know and believe that He is the perfect Covenant Keeper, the only One who will never let us down.

God Allows Needs So He Can Meet Them

Our bonds of love serve as catalysts for action on behalf of our beloveds.

I had flown down from Minnesota to be with my husband who was building a Walmart in Georgia. We were headed out for groceries and had just buckled our seatbelts when our daughter called. I barely had time to say, *"Hi Kayla!"* when I heard her sobs. I turned to look at my husband, *"She's crying."*

He turned off the truck, I put my phone on 'speaker,' and we listened as she told us through tears that she and her husband would have to move out of their rental home because the owners wanted to sell. They only had two months before having to be out.

It hadn't yet been two years since the same thing had happened to them. Their prior search for affordable housing had proven long and painful since the cost of rent had risen dramatically.

Once their friend's home had become available, though it was more than they wanted to spend, they felt they had no choice but to rent it. After they moved in, they found it suited them well, and over time, they dreamt of someday owning it.

When they were asked to leave the home they'd dreamed of owning, they didn't have the means to purchase.

And she was six weeks from the due date of their fourth little boy. *Which meant they really needed to find a place to live and move quickly.*

As I listened, faith rose up in me, and the words came with clarity, *"Honey, God knew you would be in this situation. He has never failed to provide for you. He has a plan. Let's pray."* I began to intercede:

> *"Father, Thank you that Your promises are true. You have always provided and You will not fail to meet the needs of those who trust in You. You love to show Yourself strong on behalf of Your people, Lord, please provide a home for Kayla's family. And Lord, you know they have a baby coming, and a short time to move, and because we believe nothing is impossible for you, we trust that You will make a*

> *way when there seems to be no way. And we believe you will be glorified through this. Encourage Kayla as she waits on you. In Jesus' Name, Amen."*

True to His promises, God made a way.
It is a miraculous story actually.

Unbeknown to us, my mother-in-law had finally sold a condo she'd had on the market for years. When Kayla was exploring her options, she called her grandma to see if she might cosign for a mortgage, but she found out that she would be able to purchase a home for them.

After looking at three homes, they found one in the price range they could afford, and Grandma became their mortgage lender.

They actually own their home! It suits them better than the former one, and all of it happened in a matter of weeks -- before the baby was born! God had been moving and working behind the scenes... providing for Kayla all along.

> Now to him who is able to do far more abundantly than all that we ask or think, according to the power at work within us, to him be glory in the church and in Christ Jesus throughout all generations, forever and ever. Amen. (Ephesians 3:20-21)

The bonds of family *literally* moved us all as we prayed and launched into doing the work of searching for a home, sorting, packing, painting, and ultimately helping them set up house before Baby came.

God Saves

From the time he was born in Egypt, God had his hand on Moses. His name means "drawn out," and his journey began as an allegory of God's saving grace. Due to the fact that the Egyptian King, called Pharaoh, was fearful of the rampant increase of the Israelites in the land, Pharaoh told the Hebrew midwives to kill the male babies as they assisted in delivery. (Exodus 1:15-16)

The midwives feared God more than the king of Egypt, so they did not do as instructed, and when confronted, reported that the babies were born before they arrived on the scene to help. So the king called for the boys to be thrown in the Nile river, drowning them.

When Moses was born, his mother hid him for three months. When she couldn't hide him any longer, she made a miniature ark to float him right into the palace of Pharaoh. Her brilliant plan included her ability to continue to love and nurture her son. (You can read this amazing story in Exodus 2:1-10)

Having started his life with his biological mother, Moses likely knew that he was a Hebrew even though he spent much of his life in an Egyptian palace. We can only guess what his mother told him during the years before she had to deliver him to Pharaoh's daughter. Moses knew little of trusting God, and took vengeance into his own hands.

Doing God's work man's way never fares well.

Upon confrontation by one of his fellow Israelites, the shame of this one act would turn on Moses, causing him to retreat into the wilderness.

For forty years, Moses hung out with sheep, and the Lord humbled him.

God took Moses out of Egypt in order to get Egypt out of Moses.

After all those years, Moses encounters a bush on fire one day, but he notices it is not being consumed. Curious, he approaches it, and hears God call out to him, *"Moses, Moses!"* (Drawn out, Drawn out!)

Moses answers, *"Here I am."*

> *"Do not come near; take your sandals off your feet, for the place on which you are standing is holy ground. . . . I am the God of your father, the God of Abraham, the God of Isaac, and the God of Jacob." (Exodus 3:5-6)*

God introduced Himself, and then called Moses to his specific mission. Moses would be the deliverer of God's people from slavery.

Moses, the humbled man, has such a small view of himself by this time that he quakes at the idea. God encourages him through a lengthy conversation, and by displaying His power in a way that Moses could literally touch it.

God tells Moses to throw his shepherd's staff on the ground, and it becomes a snake. God then gives Moses his power, as He directs him to take the snake "by the tail."
Moses, fearful at first, steps forward and obediently reaches out and grabs it. As he does this, it becomes a staff again.

This was a clear demonstration to Moses that God was with him. The rod was an emblem of the authority bestowed on him in that moment.

God promises to be everything Moses will need to carry out his great commission.

Moses leaves God's presence at the burning bush, and does all that God moves him to do. He leads the Israelites out of Egypt, through the waters of the Red Sea, and into their own forty year wilderness experience.

The movement seen in this story reflects God's pursuit of His family. He sets in motion all that is needed to acquire and establish His beloved ones safely in His arms.

Have you ever landed in a new location or position, and you suddenly find yourself asking, "Now what?"

Imagine this scene . . . Israel has been in slavery for four hundred years. Suddenly, their slave drivers are dead, and they're free from the pressure to serve the cruel taskmaster, but they also find themselves in a dry and weary land where there is no water.

They need their God, but they don't yet know Him. He has shown Himself through a plethora of amazing miracles. He's delivered them in every way, but can they trust His love when they find themselves in this huge caravan - in a desert, thirsty?

As God continues to meet their needs and continues to show Himself faithful by way of his faith-filled servant Moses, the Hebrew people increasingly murmur over what they don't have. As a result, they fail to see His love for them.

**How desperate we are to know
the rock-solid truth about God:
His love never fails.**

Exodus 19 - God comes down to the top of the mountain, and He calls Moses to come up to meet with Him. He establishes boundaries around the bottom of the mountain, that people should only come so far toward the Presence of God in order that He would not "break out against them" when He came to speak with them.

Exodus 20-23 - After the three days of purification, Moses leads Israel to the foot of the mountain, where they hear God give the law. The people tremble at the voice of God, and in fear, express to Moses that they want Him to bring them God's word. Moses reassures them (Ex 20:20) and God continues to give them the words that would become the Torah. Torah is the first five books in our Old Testament.

Exodus 24-31 - Moses brings his brother, Aaron and a group of priests half-way up the mountain. God then calls him higher, and he sends Aaron and the other men to go back down to govern the people. Moses is on the mountain for an extended stay of forty days receiving the tablets God Himself had cut out, and then engraved with the law.

Read Exodus 19:8-9, Exodus 20:23, and Exodus 32:1-4

> 8 All the people answered together and said, "All that the Lord has spoken we will do." And Moses reported the words of the people to the Lord. 9 And the Lord said to Moses, "Behold, I am coming to you in a thick cloud, that the people may hear when I speak with you, and may also believe you forever." Exodus 19:8-9
>
> 23 You shall not make gods of silver to be with me, nor shall you make for yourselves gods of gold. Exodus 20:23
>
> 1 When the people saw that Moses delayed to come down from the mountain, the people gathered themselves together to Aaron and said to him, "Up, make us gods who shall go before us. As for this Moses, the man who brought us up out of the land of Egypt, we do not know what has become of him." 2 So Aaron said to them, "Take off the rings of gold that are in the ears of your wives, your sons,

> and your daughters, and bring them to me." 3 So all the people took off the rings of gold that were in their ears and brought them to Aaron. 4 And he received the gold from their hand and fashioned it with a graving tool and made a golden calf. And they said, "These are your gods, O Israel, who brought you up out of the land of Egypt!" Exodus 32:1-4

Israel promises obedience, they receive instruction of what not to do, and while Moses is a long time away, they blatantly disobey.

Read the following divine conversation between Moses and God:

Read Exodus 32:7-10; 11-13:

> 7 **And the Lord said to Moses,** "Go down, for **your** people, whom **you** brought up out of the land of Egypt, have corrupted themselves. 8 They have turned aside quickly out of the way that I commanded them. They have made for themselves a golden calf and have worshiped it and sacrificed to it and said, 'These are your gods, O Israel, who brought you up out of the land of Egypt!'" 9 And the Lord said to Moses, "I have seen this people, and behold, it is a stiff-necked people. 10 Now therefore let me alone, that my wrath may burn hot against them and I may consume them, in order that I may make a great nation of you." Exodus 32:7-10[1]

> 11 **But Moses implored the Lord his God** and said, "O Lord, why does your wrath burn hot against **your** people, whom **you** have brought out of the land of Egypt with great power and with a mighty hand? 12 Why should the Egyptians say, 'With evil intent did he bring them out, to kill them in the mountains and to consume them from the face of the earth'? Turn from your burning anger and relent from this disaster against your people. 13 Remember Abraham, Isaac, and Israel, your servants, to whom you swore by your own self, and said to them, 'I will multiply your offspring as the stars of heaven, and all this land that I have promised I will give to your offspring, and they shall inherit it forever.'" Exodus 32:11-13[2]

I love that God tried to give the people to Moses, but He wouldn't have it. Moses gave them right back to God.

1
2

In this exchange, we see that because of their blatant rebellion, God was ready to annihilate all of Israel and start over with Moses.

It wouldn't be hard to imagine Moses conceding to this change of plan. Weary of the Hebrews himself, he might have responded in the affirmative, with something like, *"Wow! Okay God, if that is what You want to do. Amen and so be it!"*

But notice what happened. Moses *"implored"* the Lord by asking Him why He would do such a thing when it would give the Egyptians opportunity to accuse God of killing His people. Then he reminded God of His covenant that He made to Abraham-- to multiply his offspring and give them the land He'd promised to give to Abraham and his descendants, forever.

Keeping in mind both the covenant of God, and the intentions of God for His own glory and for His people, Moses interceded, *"And the LORD relented from the disaster that he had spoken of bringing on the people."* (Exodus 32:14)

Although many would face the wrath of God (Exodus 32:32-35) for this sin, Moses' prayer turned the wrath of God from wiping out the entire rebellious people group!

Moses' knowledge of God's will and his heart to see it carried out prompted his humble intercession. His prayer brought salvation and advancement toward home for the family of God!

What might your prayers do?

Digging Deeper

Read Exodus 32:32 to see further into the heart of Moses.

Read Romans 9:3 to see the heart of the Apostle Paul.

- **What do these men of God have in common?**

- **Who are "Your people"?**

- **Thinking of those God has given you to lead, can you relate to Moses and Paul's passion?** (If not, because our hearts often sway, you can ask God to give you His heart for them)

- **Journal some of the radical or costly things your love has caused you to do:**

Read Romans 12:1-2

- **What are the two things we are called to do?**
  -
  -

- **What will we be able to discern if we do those two things?**

Read Job 1:4-5 and summarize what you believe to be the priority of Job's heart.

Read 1 Samuel 12: 21-24 and write a prayer to God in response to what you've learned about intercession in this lesson making sure to record what you are hearing Him say to you.

God Hears Us

If you are adopted by God, your life story is also one God is writing in order to display His glory and His love for His people. He has called you to be an intercessor. He wants you to know His will. He has chosen you to pursue Him, to worship Him with your whole heart, soul, mind and strength.

God calls you to intercede

for those He's given you to lead.

Like Moses, much time is necessary to meet with God in order to know Him in such a way as to pray according to His will. Don't worry if your prayer life has suffered. We are all pursuing growth. Remember that God is the one writing your story in His timing.

There will be wilderness seasons with thirsting and testing, as well as mountaintop experiences and times when you will experience contact with God more directly. All He allows or brings into your life has purpose. He intends to get you fit for His plan for your life.

As you read the stories in these lessons, you likely have stories from your own life come to mind. Write them down, at least an outline, so that you are stewarding well what God is teaching you along the way.

We see that lonely wilderness journeys such as Moses experienced serve to humble God's children. His work in our lives displays His love and power.

Being in the wilderness with a troop of grumblers can draw us away from worship and into rebellion. Keep this in mind with those you are leading, always asking God, *"What are you up to here?"* and seek to keep in mind the bigger picture.

We need to know and believe God's word
and His covenant love.

In order to respond to God rightly,
it is good to spend time away with Him.

We will discern His will as we bear in mind
His big-picture plan.

Prayer Prompt

Precious warfare promises are found throughout scripture. A few of my favorites are Isaiah 54:17, 2 Corinthians 2:4, and Psalm 138:8 KJV. Meditate on them, (and memorize them) to use as you intercede for your people. Write a prayer for those things that concern you today.

" . . . no weapon that is fashioned against you shall succeed, and you shall refute every tongue that rises against you in judgment. This is the heritage of the servants of the Lord and their vindication from me, declares the Lord." Isaiah 54:17

But thanks be to God, who in Christ always leads us in triumphal procession, and through us spreads the fragrance of the knowledge of him everywhere. 2 Corinthians 2:14

The Lord will perfect that which concerneth me: thy mercy, O Lord, endureth for ever: forsake not the works of thine own hands. Psalm 138:8 KJV

6

NEHEMIAH

As soon as I heard these words I sat down and wept and mourned for days, and I continued fasting and praying before the God of heaven. And I said, "O Lord God of heaven, the great and awesome God who keeps covenant and steadfast love with those who love him and keep his commandments, let your ear be attentive and your eyes open, to hear the prayer of your servant that I now pray before you day and night for the people of Israel your servants...

Nehemiah 1:4-6a

*For zeal for your house has consumed me,
and the reproaches of those who reproach you have fallen on me.*

Psalm 69:9

How Does God Expect Me To Do That?

How passionate are you for the mission of God? What marks your days?

Our daily pursuits are determined by the direction we are facing. Our feet will always follow our focus. When we focus on God, we will follow Him. But when we lose that focus, we become entangled.

In our crazy, hustle-bustle society, we all have the same amount of hours in our days. Regardless of what our lives are like, we will always manage to carve out time for the things that matter to us.

We want our desires to be God's will, but we often find ourselves in over our heads, doing things that are less than His best for us -- even in ministry. The source of our distraction is usually a heart issue. If we say "yes" to someone's request for the wrong reason, we might resent it the entire time because our motive fell short of desiring to please God. If we are running ragged, trying to do all the things, we might be in pursuit of something other than Jesus.

When it comes to our spiritual life and our pursuit of God and His will, we can procrastinate, or put off the pursuit when life gets busy. We can make all kinds of choices that distract us, or even derail us. The way to get back on mission, is to turn back to the Lord. Seek His face.

It is our love for Him that will fuel our passion for His mission.

Never be lacking in zeal, but keep your spiritual fervor, serving the Lord.
Romans 12:11

I Am Desperate

My flight landed on a sunny summer Sunday near the end of July. Dale had picked me up and we were having dinner on the deck of our little lake home. The sun's reflection dancing on the water added to the peace that my heart feels when I'm home.

A text message interrupted the quiet. It was our son, Ethan. It said, *"Mom, will you please pray, Caitlin is cramping and bleeding and we are going to take her in to get checked."*

Caitlin was 20 weeks along, carrying her second baby. Immediately my mind went back to the experience my sister had when she lost her twins around the twenty-week mark of her pregnancy. I decided to go to the hospital. I knew I could never rest at home and would want to be with them if anything happened.

Perhaps my heart has never groaned so deeply in prayer. It's hard to describe the combination of fear and faith. I may have repeated the same prayers over and over, *"Dear Jesus, may Theodore be okay. Save him, please keep him in."* I pleaded with God the entire forty-minute trip.

They had already chosen his name, Theodore. It means "Gift of God." This served me large doses of hope.

Upon my arrival, I learned they had done an ultrasound, and the cramping had ceased. Being uncertain of what was happening with Caitlin, the doctor sent her home on 'pelvic rest' – I was available to spend the following day with her and their one year old, Oliver.

Things seemed quiet all day. When Ethan returned from work, I left for home. Shortly past midnight, I woke to my phone ringing next to my head. *"Mom, can you come and stay with Oliver, Caitlin is cramping and we are going in again."*

In a flash, with bags still packed from the conference, I threw them in my four-wheeled rocket, and landed the 40-minute trip within a half an hour.

This midnight call repeated two more times between Sunday and the following Saturday. We all but lost track of what day it was. Events are blurry due to lack of sleep and heightened emotions, but it was Saturday when the Lord put on my heart to call our pastor and have him come and pray over Caitlin.

The intensity of my prayers in this battle is unmatched at this point in my life. As fears cropped up during the ten days of intermittent "sparks of hope" amidst my urgent pleading, I pressed into God for His mercy and grace.

One of my greatest fears landed hard on me about five days in. It had suddenly occurred to me that Ethan and Caitlin might get mad at God and turn away from Him if He chose not to keep Theodore in the womb. **I pleaded for their faith not to fail.**

When Pastor arrived with two others, he opened his Bible and began to read; it was the exact passage in Isaiah 41 that I had read on the phone as I prayed with Caitlin. It was God's voice that I heard in the room, *"When you walk through the waters, I will be with you."*

My heart took pleasure in the peace and comfort of God's presence with us. We prayed in a circle around Caitlin's bed, and when it was Ethan's turn, I heard him surrender everything to God, declaring trust in His sovereignty, and his willingness to accept God's will, whatever that would be.

I felt like prostrating myself right there in my intense gratitude for that moment. Internally, I was laid out flat, face on the floor.

Theo was born on the following Tuesday, and died right away because he was just a week too early to save. If I were to tell of all of the ways God ministered to us in that painful journey, I'd be writing chapters on a woman's zealous prayers and a God who hears and answers – all according to His perfect will.

God answered every single prayer but one.

There is no greater comfort in a time like that, than knowing God is sovereign. There is no greater joy, even in pain, than to know *He is with us*.

Your deepest desires fuel your prayers.

God Strengthens

The Jews had been exiled from their home in Jerusalem. For seventy years they had lived in pagan Babylon before God elevated Cyrus, King of Persia, as His agent of restoration.

King Cyrus decreed that he had been charged to *"build God a house at Jerusalem in Judah."* (See Ezra 1:1-3)

In the first wave of the Jews returning to Jerusalem, Zerubbabel led the rebuilding of the temple, thus reestablishing praise in the house of God. (Ezra 1-6)

Once the Temple was finished and dedicated, Ezra led God's people through confession and repentance. (Ezra 7-10)

On the heels of their repentance, God stirs Nehemiah's heart to pursue the huge task of rebuilding the wall surrounding Jerusalem.

Listen carefully to how Nehemiah responds to the report brought to him by his brother, Hinani, and some other men from Judah:

Read Nehemiah 1:5-11:

> 5 And I said, "O LordGod of heaven, the great and awesome God who keeps covenant and steadfast love with those who love him and keep his commandments, 6 let your ear be attentive and your eyes open, to hear the prayer of your servant that I now pray before you day and night for the people of Israel your servants, confessing the sins of the people of Israel, which we have sinned against you. Even I and my father's house have sinned. 7 We have acted very corruptly against you and have not kept the commandments, the statutes, and the rules that you commanded your servant Moses. 8 Remember the word that you commanded your servant Moses, saying, 'If you are unfaithful, I will scatter you among the peoples, 9 but if you return to me and keep my commandments and do them, though your outcasts are in the uttermost parts of heaven, from there I will gather them and bring them to the place that I have chosen, to make my name dwell there.' 10 They are your servants and your people, whom you have redeemed by your great power and by your strong hand. 11 O Lord, let your ear be attentive to the prayer of your servant, and to the prayer of your servants who delight to fear your name, and give success to your servant today, and grant him mercy in the sight of this man."
>
> Now I was cupbearer to the king.

Scripture doesn't tell us why Nehemiah reacted to the news with such a devoted spirit, since he had never known Jerusalem as his home, but it's safe to conclude that he had an intimate relationship with God. We can see his familiarity with God's word and His work within his prayer. He probably cried out to God for his own family, whom he'd been separated from, and God placed his divine zeal within Nehemiah's heart for the welfare of His people.

We can imagine him yearning to receive news of his family.

Nehemiah's zeal for God's people appears to be no less than mine was-- that of a grandmother who is pleading for the life of her grandson.

This is about family.

Zeal is defined as, *"Fervor in advancing a cause or rendering service."* In scripture it can also mean *"God's jealous concern for His people or their welfare."* The word "Passionate" can be synonymous with the word zealous.

Four months after Nehemiah received the news about Jerusalem, he was summoned to take wine to the King. The King noticed Nehemiah's face was unusually sad, and asked him for the reason.

Nehemiah, very much afraid, tells the King that the wall around the city of his fathers lies in ruins and its gates have been burned.

"What are you requesting?" asked the King.

In response, Nehemiah shoots up a prayer before he asks the King if he would allow him to go to Jerusalem and rebuild the wall.

Read Nehemiah 2:6-87

> And I said to the king, "If it pleases the king, let letters be given me to the governors of the province Beyond the River, that they may let me pass through until I come to Judah, 8 and a letter to Asaph, the keeper of the king's forest, that he may give me timber to make beams for the gates of the fortress of the temple, and for the wall of the city, and for the house that I shall occupy." And the king granted me what I asked, for the good hand of my God was upon me.

What a glorious display of God's abundant provision in response to earnest prayer! Nehemiah approached the King, who obviously had a soft heart toward Nehemiah since he asked him about his reason for sadness. But the overabundant supplies he was willing to send with Nehemiah speak of a move of God on the heart of a King.

The King granted him:

- Letters to governors for safe passage through the land.
- A letter for the king's keeper-of-trees to provide all the lumber he'd need for the gates of the Temple, the wall, and for a house for Nehemiah.

This is certainly no small project God has laid on Nehemiah's heart!

Additionally, as Nehemiah heads out, he has been provided officers of the army and horses to accompany him on his journey.

The favor of God is so clearly displayed in the King's generosity. How do you think God's abundant provision served Nehemiah as he set out on the journey and faced such a large task?

The rest of the saga is compelling, with all the elements of a great story. Villains, intrigue, and opposition never stop this praying man from carrying out the work of God. Trials and hardships did not stop him from completing the task he'd set out to do.

Digging Deeper

Following the traditional pattern of Jewish Rabbinical training, (A Rabbi is an official Jewish teacher) Jesus was established as a Rabbi – it was required that Rabbis be confirmed by two voices of Rabbinical authority. It happened at His baptism, which marked the beginning of His public ministry.

John the Baptist and God the Father were the two voices confirming Jesus.

John the Baptizer said, "*This is the Son of God.*" And God the Father said, *"This is my Son, with whom I am well pleased."* Being the Son of God gave Him all authority.

Of the four gospels, John is the only one that records what scholars agree is likely a different incident of Jesus cleansing the temple by turning over the tables of the moneychangers -- at the beginning of his ministry. The other three gospels tell a similar story as Jesus approaches the cross.

Please open your Bible and read John 2:13-17 and Mark 11:15-17 (Of the three gospels, Mark's story has the most detail. *The other passages are Matthew 21:12-13 and Luke 19:45-46***)**

- **What are your first thoughts regarding the reason for Jesus' actions in these passages?**

It is important to notice that prayers in scripture are based on God's promises and truths found in His word. The language of the New Testament writers reflected the language of the Old Testament and brought scripture forward.

As a Rabbi, Jesus was intimately acquainted with scripture. He did not carry around a Bible like we do, but instead memorized, diligently, the first five books of the Old Testament before the age of twelve. If we recall the story of his boyhood, the time when his mother and father accidentally left him behind in Jerusalem, we might surmise by the way they found him among the Rabbis who were marveling at his understanding, that he had memorized much more than was required of him.

Let's look at the two passages surrounding the verses Jesus quoted, Jeremiah 7:9-15 and then Isaiah 56:1-7, in order to see what Jesus was saying during his zealous table turning.

Look up Jeremiah 7:8-15

- **How does Jeremiah describe the actions of the recipients of his message?**

- **The people come into God's house boldly saying "We are delivered!" but God clarifies what they are really doing. What does He call their actions?**

- **What does God say is the root of their sin problem in verse 13?**

- **Considering Jesus quoted verse 11 from this passage regarding the moneychangers, what would He have been angry about?**

Write a prayer for your own time with the Lord, asking Him to increase your prayer life, enable your ear to be more in tune with His voice, and for anything else you need to deepen your love for Him.

Look up Isaiah 56:1-7

- **Circle or highlight the words "keep" and "hold".**
- **Who is Isaiah referring to in the beginning of verse 7, which begins with *"these"?***
- **What is God delighted to do for them? (Verses 7-8)**
- **Finish this sentence: "My house shall be called . . .**
- **What do you believe Jesus is so fervent to protect and why?**

God Stokes Us

The zeal of the Lord is made crystal clear -- if our eyes are open. We see it through the passion of our Lord Jesus Christ, displayed on the cross, and we see it in his passion for the purpose of the House of God.

During His ministry on earth, Jesus displayed His fervent love for God's will, and for the redemption of God's people. His great desire was and continues to be-- adding on to His Family. Jesus was zealous as He turned the tables of the money changers who were preventing true worship.

True worship can essentially be described as intimacy with God. His redeemed people who are in relationship with Him, and who listen to His word and talk with Him. Prayer is evidence of the fruit of His cross.

Nehemiah's life is an example of one who truly worshiped God. His worship was demonstrated through his fervent prayer for God's people, through his courage, and in his power to get the job done.

The lengths God was willing to go to redeem us from Satan, sin, and death, speak of His fiery, radical love. The same love that He pours into our hearts by the Spirit at conversion.

As redeemed children, our zeal for building the Kingdom of God should reflect His. Our own fervor will be acquired through our fellowship with Him. No wonder He wants us to pray!

Jesus is zealous for reconciliation
between God and His family.

True worship is an ongoing divine conversation.

Zeal for God's house is acquired
through our intimacy with Him.

Prayer Prompt

Pen a prayer to God about your own life, offering it afresh to Him. Ask for His grace to help you wait upon Him with anticipation for His hand to bless and favor you. Pray for Him to give you His zeal for His work through your life. Pray that He will make you a woman of prayer.

For zeal for your house has consumed me, and the reproaches of those who reproach you have fallen on me.
Psalm 69:9

For we are his workmanship, created in Christ Jesus for good works, which God prepared beforehand, that we should walk in them.
Ephesians 2:10

SOLOMON

power & presence & pleasure

"O Lord, God of Israel, there is no God like you, in heaven or on earth, keeping covenant and showing steadfast love to your servants who walk before you with all their heart . . .

"But will God indeed dwell with man on the earth? Behold, heaven and the highest heaven cannot contain you, how much less this house that I have built!

And listen to the pleas of your servant and of your people Israel, when they pray toward this place. And listen from heaven your dwelling place, and when you hear, forgive.

2 Chronicles 6:14, 18, 21

Now my eyes will be open and my ears attentive to the prayers offered in this place. I have chosen and consecrated this temple so that my Name may be there forever. My eyes and my heart will always be there.

2 Chronicles 7:15-16

Does God Care About Details?

One Sunday, a woman in our Sunday School class asked if God really cared about whether she chose peanut butter or turkey sandwich for lunch. Another was a little miffed that people actually pray for a close parking place at the mall. *"God doesn't care about things like that! He has more important things to do!"* she said.

Oswald Chambers says, "When you are rightly related to God, it is a life of freedom and liberty and delight, you *are* God's will, and all your common sense decisions are His will for you unless He checks. (From 3/20 entry in My Utmost For His Highest) In other words, enjoy your peanut butter unless the Holy Spirit tells you otherwise.

We often have wrong concepts of God when we begin our relationship with Him. He loves to make Himself known as we walk with Him.

If we are pressed for time and need to swing into the mall for something, we absolutely should ask our Father for a close parking spot. He delights to give good gifts to His children. He also delights when His children ask Him for things with confident expectation. Often the missing link between us and our need is the tiny word, "ask". If this is true, imagine how He responds to us when we ask together!

If you then, who are evil, know how to give good gifts to your children, how much more will the heavenly Father give the Holy Spirit to those who ask him!"
(Luke 11:13)

God wants to fill us with Himself.

What more could we ever ask of Him?

I Forget To Pray

Hurricane Katrina hit New Orleans in the summer of 2005. Nearly a year later, in July of 2006, our church and a sister church we did ministry with rented a tour-bus and three large vans. We headed down on a sunny July day with our youth groups to serve the Lord. Our ministry would include gutting and cleaning houses, visiting with hurricane victims, street witnessing, and hosting a Vacation Bible School (VBS) for children in a local apartment courtyard.

We prepared our skits for VBS over the preceding weeks, as well as our hearts through a study of the gospel of Luke. With our air mattresses, sleeping bags, and duffel bags filled with work clothes, we loaded up and headed out. Twenty hours or so later, we unpacked and set up camp on the floor of the host church.

My group anticipated impressing children with our well-rehearsed skits on the first day, a Monday. Goliath donned his costume, David stood upon a short landscape wall with his sling and stone. We gave it all we had, but there was so much noise and chaos, it was as if hurricane winds had completely drowned out our voices. Not a word we'd spoken was heard.

It felt like a waste.

I left VBS very discouraged. We'd worked so hard to get our lines down, had such high hopes of seeing faces light up, but it felt like the lollipops and ice cream were the highlights of the day to the kids who attended.

The next morning, I was scheduled to give the devotion to the whole gang before setting off on the bus for the VBS courtyard. I woke early in order to sneak away by myself.

Sitting in a corner with my Bible in my lap, I inhaled deeply as my eyes landed on this passage:

> In these days he (Jesus) went out to the mountain to pray, and all night he continued in prayer to God. And when day came, he called his disciples and chose from them twelve, whom he named apostles. (Luke 6:12-13)

It struck me. Jesus Himself prayed ALL NIGHT before choosing His disciples. I was immediately aware of the fact that our entire trip had been altogether prayerless. *We'd forgotten the most important thing!*

I knew right away what the Lord wanted me to talk to the group about.

As leaders we were "cut to the heart" for our prayerlessness, and as a result, the Pastor asked me to lead prayer when we got on the bus. I had the students huddle and pray in their seats.

The resulting contrast in Tuesday's VBS was marked, and with more prayer, Wednesday's was like night and day. The entire ninety minutes was miraculously orderly in contrast to Monday's attempt. The children heard and responded to the stories with enthusiasm *and* enjoyed their treats.

God showed up because we prayed. There is no other explanation for the drastic difference we experienced.

We would be wise to push pause on our lives - often - and take inventory of all of the things we are doing in the name of Jesus. We might make a regular assessment of whether our pursuits are undergirded with prayer. It's possible we are spinning our wheels, but gaining very little traction because we have failed to invite God's power supply through prayer.

> The sacrifice of the wicked is an abomination to the Lord, but the prayer of the upright is his delight. (Proverbs 15:8)

Does God know you to be a woman of prayer?

If the answer is "no" or "maybe," *please do not be discouraged* -- you are not alone. If we would ask the question in any great assembly of Christians, *"Are you content and satisfied with your prayer life?"* It would be shocking to ever hear a "yes." We all need to grow in this pursuit.

God Comes

"The first established meeting place for God and His people was the Tabernacle during the Israelites' wilderness wandering. The design for the Tabernacle was given by God to Moses and carried out with precision. It was to be the place of meeting and the evidence of God's presence with His people.

After the wandering nation of Israel was at home in the Promised Land, and David was established as King, he had it in his heart to build a "house for God" to dwell among them. However, when he inquired of God about building it, he was prevented since he had been a man of bloodshed.

In His mercy, God gave him the design and enabled him to gather supplies to be given to his successor. With the instructions for building, David's son, Solomon, carried out the design with precision until finally dedicating it to the Lord at its completion. (2 Chronicles 7:11)

The Temple was precious to both God and His people as a meeting place and an emblem of His presence." (excerpt from Kathy's study, **dearly BeLoved,** chapter 7)

Solomon's prayer of dedication of the Temple might be one of the longest prayers in the Bible.

We find it twice in the Old Testament. First in 1 Kings 8:23-61, and then in 2 Chronicles 6:14-42. There are slight expansions in the Chronicles prayer, which is the reason we are focusing our attention there.

Read 2 Chronicles 6:7-21:

> 7 Now it was in the heart of David my father to build a house for the name of the Lord, the God of Israel. 8 But the Lord said to David my father, 'Whereas it was in your heart to build a house for my name, you did well that it was in your heart.9 Nevertheless, it is not you who shall build the house, but your son who shall be born to you shall build the house for my name.' 10 Now the Lord has fulfilled his promise that he made. For I have risen in the place of David my father and sit on the throne of Israel, as the Lord

promised, and I have built the house for the name of the Lord, the God of Israel. 11 And there I have set the ark, in which is the covenant of the Lord that he made with the people of Israel."

12 Then Solomon stood before the altar of the Lord in the presence of all the assembly of Israel and spread out his hands. 13 Solomon had made a bronze platform five cubits long, five cubits wide, and three cubits high, and had set it in the court, and he stood on it. Then he knelt on his knees in the presence of all the assembly of Israel, and spread out his hands toward heaven, 14 and said, "O Lord, God of Israel, there is no God like you, in heaven or on earth, keeping covenant and showing steadfast love to your servants who walk before you with all their heart, 15 who have kept with your servant David my father what you declared to him. You spoke with your mouth, and with your hand have fulfilled it this day.16 Now therefore, O Lord, God of Israel, keep for your servant David my father what you have promised him, saying, 'You shall not lack a man to sit before me on the throne of Israel, if only your sons pay close attention to their way, to walk in my law as you have walked before me.' 17 Now therefore, O Lord, God of Israel, let your word be confirmed, which you have spoken to your servant David.

18 "But will God indeed dwell with man on the earth? Behold, heaven and the highest heaven cannot contain you, how much less this house that I have built!19 Yet have regard to the prayer of your servant and to his plea, O Lord my God, listening to the cry and to the prayer that your servant prays before you, 20 that your eyes may be open day and night toward this house, the place where you have promised to set your name, that you may listen to the prayer that your servant offers toward this place. 21 **And listen to the pleas of your servant and of your people Israel, when they pray toward this place. And listen from heaven your dwelling place, and when you hear, forgive.**[1]

1

Upon completion of the temple, the people of God were doing what the people of God often do, though their potlucks were likely of a different variety. Regardless of their lack of cream of mushroom soup, they are gathered together to dedicate and celebrate.

King Solomon steps up to the bronze platform he built, spreads out his hands, and after what might have been a significant pause, gets down on his knees. With his hands still raised, he opens his prayer, *"O Lord, God of Israel,"* and he declares Him to be a covenant-keeper. He praises God for fulfilling His promise that He'd spoken "by His mouth, and fulfilled by His hand," the promise to his father, David, that his son would build the Temple.

This was *the day*.
They are living *in the moment* of a fulfilled promise.

Pause and think of that! Have you ever had such a moment, when you are suddenly aware of the presence and power of God breaking through with fulfillment of His promise?

In all of our day to day doings, in our mundane Monday moments, and in our freaky Friday fodder, God is just a prayer away.

As born-again believers in Jesus, who've been given the Spirit of God to dwell inside of us, our bodies are the New Covenant Temple. Heaven is as close to us while we are folding laundry as it is when we are gathered in sacred assemblies.

Listen intently, feeling Solomon's emotion, as you hear these words of Solomon's prayer one more time, (Read them with perceived emotion.) -- from 2 Chronicles 6:18:

> But will God indeed dwell with man on the earth? Behold, heaven and the highest heaven cannot contain You, how much less this house that I have built!

He seems astonished. He might have been breathless!

Listen to what 1 Corinthians 3:16 tells us about you and me:

> Don't you know that you yourselves are God's temple and that God's Spirit dwells in your midst?

Does that make *you* breathless?

When is the last time you marveled at the divine honor bestowed upon YOU, chosen and adopted child of God? The King of Heaven lives in you!

Now, think about this: When we who are containers of the Holy Spirit come together in large numbers, the presence and the experience of God's glory increases.

The larger the gathering of flames,
the brighter and hotter the fire!

God's house shall be called a house of prayer for all people, and true worshippers will worship in spirit and in truth.

In his prayer of dedication for God's house, Solomon ends the first portion that we read earlier -- in verse 21 with *". . . and when you hear, forgive."*

Then He continues his prayer with, "When . . . when a man sins by lying, when a man sins by turning away from God . . . and after having felt the consequences of their sins, they turn back to God in repentance, and pray toward the Temple:

Solomon prays, *"then hear from Heaven, and forgive, and relent from Your punishment."*
(2 Chronicles 6:22-39)

Hear, and forgive.
Hear and forgive.
Hear and forgive. (He repeats this phrase three times, in verses 25, 27, and 30)

Don't miss this: We find the word "prayer" in its various forms, no less than 16 times in this lengthy supplication.

Solomon is dedicating the Temple as none other than a "House of Prayer."

The Temple of God is a house of reconciliation and communication, a house for the children to have communion with their Father. Don't we have hints of God's intent within the four walls of our own homes?

God's Temple is Family Dining at its Divinest.

Let's look at God's response to Solomon's long prayer.

Read 2 Chronicles 7:1-3:

> 1 As soon as Solomon finished his prayer, fire came down from heaven and consumed the burnt offering and the sacrifices, and the glory of the Lord filled the temple. 2 And the priests could not enter the house of the Lord, because the glory of the Lord filled the Lord's house. 3 When all the people of Israel saw the fire come down and the glory of the Lord on the temple, they bowed down with their faces to the ground on the pavement and worshiped and gave thanks to the Lord, saying, "For he is good, for his steadfast love endures forever."

Have you ever seen anything like it?!!

- Maybe at the reception of the war-hero who returns from combat alive and well.
- Perhaps when Grandpa opens the door and his grandsons come running into his arms, yelling, *"Grampa!!!!"*
- Maybe a standing ovation at a live musical performance that strikes your heart and blows your mind.

After this prayer of Solomon, God's presence blazes so fierce that no one can come near! His glory fills the Temple! Nothing could keep Him away from this house that took so much planning, effort, attention and skill!

The house of God is suddenly inhabited by the praise and prayers of His beloved people!

This Dwelling was built with great anticipation of having the presence of God physically accessible to humanity. Immanuel, God With Us.

King David's desire was to have God as near as possible. God hasn't missed one second of the hard work that has been invested in His house. The same is true of you. Not a cup of cold water given to one of His little ones will go unnoticed or fail to be rewarded in Heaven. With God, there are no mundane Monday moments. Every ounce of your faithful love will be counted.

It is what we all crave. God craves this most of all.

God longs for us to crave Him!

His presence was so profound, they all fell on the ground - it says, *“faces to the ground in the pavement, they worshipped and gave thanks to God.” Hallelujah!*

Digging Deeper

Can you think of a time when you were desperate for prayer and someone prayed over you and you saw the hand of God move on your behalf? (Or your prayer was answered for someone?)

In the days of the early church, King Herod “laid violent hands on some who belonged to the church. He killed James, the brother of John with the sword and when he saw that it pleased the Jews, he proceeded to arrest Peter also.” (Acts 12:1-3a)

He arrested and imprisoned Peter, putting him under the watch of four squads of guards.

Complete the sentence from Acts 12:5 below:

- **So Peter was kept in prison, but ________________ prayer ___________________ __________________________ to God by ________________________.**

Read Acts 12: 6-11

- **Describe Peter's circumstances in verse 6:**

- **What happened in verses 7-9?**

During this miracle, Peter thought he was sleeping, and as soon as the angel left him, scripture says, "Peter came to himself" and expressed his certainty that he'd been rescued by Jesus. He proceeded to go to the house of Mary, the mother of John (Mark) where many were gathered together praying. And when he knocked at the door of the gateway, a servant girl named Rhoda came to answer. (Acts 12:12-13)

Read Acts 12:12-19

We are told "many" of the church were gathered at Mary's house praying when Rhoda, the servant girl came to answer Peter's knock. What did she do instead of opening the gate for him?

- **How did the praying saints respond? (verse 15)**

- **Peter continued knocking and when they opened they were ____________.** (verse 16)

We can likely relate with the surprised response to the miracle witnessed by the praying group.

- **Can you think of a time when you were shocked when God answered a prayer?**

- **How is your heart being stirred for prayer during this Bible study so far?**

- **What steps are you going to take to increase your prayer life?**

Go back and read verse 19.

- **Who did Herod kill instead of Peter?**

- **The tables turned on the oppressor. Does this remind you of any other stories from scripture?**

If you aren't familiar with the story of the evil Haman and humble Mordecai from the book of Esther, you could go read the short book right now. It is a compelling story! But if you don't have time, take a peek at the table-turning God does through the faith of His people in Esther 3:5-6, 9, and Esther 5:9-14, and Esther 7:9-10. Marvel at the way God turned the wrath of the enemy on his own evil neck.

- **How has this week's study changed how you perceive prayer and God's love for your presence?**

God Wants Us Home In Him

Even our noblest pursuits, without prayer, will lack power and order. Conversely, our weakest pursuits undergirded with prayer will reap eternal riches. Like any good parent, when His child cries out, He moves Heaven and Earth to come to our rescue.

We are up against the world, our flesh, and the devil when it comes to spending time on our knees. Knowing how passionate God is to be united with us in every detail serves as motivation to push past roadblocks.

When we understand what prayer is -- communion with God -- and how significant it is to His mission on the earth and the work that He calls us to, we will discipline ourselves more intently.

If we remember how much pleasure our prayer brings Him and how His presence becomes more evident in our gatherings, we will make time to meet with other believers to experience His love and power. Spending time together will help us be more effective in our disciple-making mission.

God takes great pleasure
in the prayers of His people.

God will move heaven and earth
to come to us when we call.

Power for God's work is activated when His people
gather in the House of Prayer.

Prayer Prompt

Ask the Holy Spirit if there is anything between you and Him, then pen a prayer of repentance for anything He brings to mind. Express your thanksgiving for His forgiveness and His cleansing blood. Praise Him with jubilation (if you aren't familiar with that word, look it up in a dictionary) **for making His home in you.**

"In returning and rest you shall be saved; in quietness and in trust shall be your strength."
Isaiah 30:15

If we confess our sins, he is faithful and just to forgive us our sins and to cleanse us from all unrighteousness. 1 John 1:9

"But will God indeed dwell with man on the earth? Behold, heaven and the highest heaven cannot contain you, how much less this house . . . !
2 Chronicles 6:18

But the angel said to him, "Do not be afraid, Zechariah, for your prayer has been heard, and your wife Elizabeth will bear you a son, and you shall call his name John.
Luke 1:13

And Zechariah said to the angel, "How shall I know this? For I am an old man, and my wife is advanced in years."
Luke 1:18

For the gifts and the calling of God are irrevocable.
Romans 11:29

When Will God Move The Mountain?

There are times in our lives when God surprises us with an "AHA!"-- an awareness of an answer to a prayer appears seemingly out of nowhere. It might be a long-forgotten prayer, one prayed in the distant past, or it could be a request prayed in the morning and answered by noon.

In our surprise, we might respond one of two ways. Our reaction could be a joyful, faithful expression of praise, or it could be one of stark unbelief. Zechariah experienced this when the Angel of the Lord showed up one day in the gospel of Luke to announce, "Your prayer has been heard."

We saw in chapter one of this study that both Abram and Sarai laughed at the Lord's announcement of them conceiving and giving birth to a son when they were five decades past childbearing age. Can you picture God laughing with joy in His own mercy and goodness, when the day finally came that the two of them could hardly contain their elation that Isaac was born? We will look at Zechariah and Elizabeth's story now and see how it reflects theirs in several ways.

When I Pray

It was only a few years after I'd made an ongoing request, when the Lord surprised me.

I was attending a reception with many mothers who were actively part of Mom's In Touch Internationall[1] (MITI). The ministry founder, Fern Nichols, along with local members of the organization had been invited to meet an upcoming evangelist. Nick Hall is the founder of the Pulse Movement[2] based in Minneapolis, MN.

Acknowledging that his mom's prayers were foundational to him hearing the call from God, Nick had reached out to gather us for a reception. He introduced himself and informed us of the event Pulse was hosting on the National Day of Prayer which would take place at the Mariucci Arena, on the U of M campus.

Nick testified of having spent regular concentrated time alone with Jesus in a small sanctuary on his college campus in prayer.

1
2

Following the season of conversions with God, he'd written a paper on his growing desire to make Jesus the pulse of a generation.

Shortly after, God made it clear that he was to leave the college he was attending and "go" with his mission to the campus of North Dakota State University.

North Dakota . . . NDSU . . . the letters rang in my memory. My brother had previously attended there, and as I would pray for him during those years, one recurring request continued to come from my lips. "Lord, send a worker into the harvest field of NDSU."

I had prayed that prayer weekly.

After hearing the year in which Nick wrote his paper, I quickly did the math, recalling which years my brother attended NDSU - and then the surprise came.

The Lord spoke clearly to my heart, "This is the one you were praying for."

One of my dearest friends happened to be a friend of Nick's mom. She began to work as Nick's personal secretary. Through those connections, I received an invitation to be on the intercessory prayer team for the Pulse Movement.

In my heart, because of the answered prayer, I sort of adopted Nick. I felt called to keep praying for him. In the last several years, It's been amazing to watch God continue to beautifully answer our prayers for Nick and for the ministry of the Pulse Movement.

God Surprises

I read somewhere that it was the hope of every Jewish mother that her child might be the key to Israel's future. This hope might help explain Mary's faith-filled reaction to the announcement of Gabriel when he visited her with the news that she was chosen to bear the Son of the Most High.

Throughout scripture, we read of barren women whose hearts ached in their longing for children. Culturally, having children was a woman's crown, especially if she was given male children. As a woman, if you were barren, you were considered inferior which often resulted in being ostracized.

I love that the Christmas story centers on two women and their husbands, each person having a unique role in the story of Jesus coming to be with us.

Read Luke 1:5-38

> 5 In the days of Herod, king of Judea, there was a priest named Zechariah, of the division of Abijah. And he had a wife from the daughters of Aaron, and her name was Elizabeth. 6 And they were both righteous before God, walking blamelessly in all the commandments and statutes of the Lord. 7 But they had no child, because Elizabeth was barren, and both were advanced in years.
>
> 8 Now while he was serving as priest before God when his division was on duty,9 according to the custom of the priesthood, he was chosen by lot to enter the temple of the Lord and burn incense. 10 And the whole multitude of the people were praying outside at the hour of incense. 11 And there appeared to him an angel of the Lord standing on the right side of the altar of incense. 12 And Zechariah was troubled when he saw him, and fear fell upon him. 13 But the angel said to him, "Do not be afraid, Zechariah, for your prayer has been heard, and your wife Elizabeth will bear you a son, and you shall call his name John. 14 And you will have joy and gladness, and many will rejoice at his birth, 15 for he will be great before the Lord. And he must not drink wine or strong drink, and he will be filled with the Holy Spirit, even from his mother's womb. 16 And he will turn many of the children of Israel to the Lord their God, 17 and he will go before him in the spirit and power of Elijah, to turn the hearts of the fathers to the children, and the disobedient to the wisdom of the just, to make ready for the Lord a people prepared."
>
> 18 And Zechariah said to the angel, "How shall I know this? For I am an old man, and my wife is advanced in years." 19 And the angel answered him, "I am Gabriel. I stand in the presence of God, and I was sent to speak to you and to bring you this good news. 20 And behold, you will be silent and unable to speak until the day that these things take place, because you did not believe my words, which will be fulfilled in their time." 21 And the people were

waiting for Zechariah, and they were wondering at his delay in the temple. 22 And when he came out, he was unable to speak to them, and they realized that he had seen a vision in the temple. And he kept making signs to them and remained mute. 23 And when his time of service was ended, he went to his home.

24 After these days his wife Elizabeth conceived, and for five months she kept herself hidden, saying, 25 "Thus the Lord has done for me in the days when he looked on me, to take away my reproach among people."

26 In the sixth month the angel Gabriel was sent from God to a city of Galilee named Nazareth, 27 to a virgin betrothed to a man whose name was Joseph, of the house of David. And the virgin's name was Mary. 28 And he came to her and said, "Greetings, O favored one, the Lord is with you!" 29 But she was greatly troubled at the saying, and tried to discern what sort of greeting this might be. 30 And the angel said to her, "Do not be afraid, Mary, for you have found favor with God.31 And behold, you will conceive in your womb and bear a son, and you shall call his name Jesus. 32 He will be great and will be called the Son of the Most High. And the Lord God will give to him the throne of his father David, 33 and he will reign over the house of Jacob forever, and of his kingdom there will be no end."

34 And Mary said to the angel, "How will this be, since I am a virgin?"

35 And the angel answered her, "The Holy Spirit will come upon you, and the power of the Most High will overshadow you; therefore the child to be born will be called holy—the Son of God. 36 And behold, your relative Elizabeth in her old age has also conceived a son, and this is the sixth month with her who was called barren. 37 For nothing will be impossible with God." 38 And Mary said, "Behold, I am the servant of the Lord; let it be to me according to your word." And the angel departed from her.

Likely Elizabeth ached for years, agonizing in prayer, along with her husband Zechariah, for a child. By the time the angel showed up, they were long past any hope of bearing a son; they'd given up on their dream all together. There is no suggestion that there was a promise made to them, like the one God had given to Abraham, that they should cling to hope as he and Sarah had.
Scripture isn't clear regarding which prayer of Zechariah the

angel was referring to. We could assume, based on the reported forthcoming answer, that it was the prayer-of-his-life over the duration of his marriage to Elizabeth. It could also have been a prayer he prayed that very day as he was offering incense. Perhaps priests regularly prayed for Messiah to show up when they entered into the holy place, and that was what the angel of the Lord was referring to.

We might conclude that it was one or the other, or maybe both. *What do you think?*

As we look at this divine conversation between the angel of the Lord and Zechariah, we cannot miss the first details regarding the couple that would bear the prophesied forerunner to Christ. (See John 3:28) We are told both Zechariah and Elizabeth were descendants of Aaron, of the chosen priestly line, and they are described in verse six as being "righteous in the sight of God, walking blamelessly in all the commandments and requirements of the Lord."

Two verses of scripture come to mind here:

> The prayer of a righteous person has great power as it is working. (James 5:16b)
>
> If I had not confessed the sin in my heart, the Lord would not have listened. (Psalm 66:18 NLT)

We want our prayers to impact our neighborhoods, cities, country and the world for eternity. As women who seek to pursue the Lord for our deepest desires, we must begin at the beginning – with our hearts.

A righteous person whose prayers are powerful and effective is simply one who has repented of her sin, and whose sin is covered by the blood of Jesus.

A righteous person is NOT a person who never sins, but one who agrees with God about her sin. She literally hates her sin, and repents every time she becomes aware of its stain in her life. The righteousness of Christ is imputed to her.

This is cause for great celebration as well as anticipation of our prayers being heard and answered.
We get to actively participate in building the Kingdom of God!

Before moving on in the story of Zechariah and Elizabeth, let's pause and look at a few other promises from Jesus found in John's gospel regarding the prayers of the righteous:
Read John 14:13, John 15:7, John 15:16, John 16:23:

> Whatever you ask in my name, this I will do, that the Father may be glorified in the Son. (John 14:13)
>
> If you abide in me, and my words abide in you, ask whatever you wish, and it will be done for you. (John 15:7)
>
> You did not choose me, but I chose you and appointed you that you should go and bear fruit and that your fruit should abide, so that whatever you ask the Father in my name, he may give it to you. (John 15:16)
>
> In that day you will ask nothing of me. Truly, truly, I say to you, whatever you ask of the Father in my name, he will give it to you. (John 16:23)

I hope you noticed the absolutes in these verses. Whatever you ask - I will do - it will be done for you . . . there is no indication of a maybe in any of those promises. In saying this, it is important to note that growing in our knowledge of God and His will through His word is essential in approaching Him with confidence for the "Yes" and the "Amen" that has been promised.

The Apostle Paul tells us in Romans that we who belong to the Lord are to offer our bodies as living sacrifices to God, and that our minds are to be transformed and renewed by His word. In so doing, we gain an understanding of the good, pleasant and perfect will of God. (Romans 12:1-2)

Simply stated, we must be in an intimate, ongoing relationship with the Lord for His purposes to be brought to fruition in our lives.

When we pray, even though most of us won't be visited by an angel, the Holy Spirit will speak to us as we sit with Him, walk with Him, and do all of life abiding in Him and His word.

The place Zechariah stood the day the angel shocked him was in the very presence of God.

It was a moment he had waited with anticipation for all of his life. His name had been chosen by lot, the ancient method of "drawing straws," to be the one to offer incense to the Lord in the sanctuary. This event only occurred once a year and you could only be chosen for the role once in your lifetime.

Zechariah had one final duty after leaving God's presence in the temple. He was to bless the people who had been outside praying.

(Luke 1:21) But, due to his unbelief, he was unable to do so. Then, look what happens after the baby is born:

Read Luke 1:57-68

57 Now the time came for Elizabeth to give birth, and she bore a son. 58 And her neighbors and relatives heard that the Lord had shown great mercy to her, and they rejoiced with her. 59 And on the eighth day they came to circumcise the child. And they would have called him Zechariah after his father, 60 but his mother answered, "No; he shall be called John." 61 And they said to her, "None of your relatives is called by this name." 62 And they made signs to his father, inquiring what he wanted him to be called. 63 And he asked for a writing tablet and wrote, "His name is John." And they all wondered. 64 And immediately his mouth was opened and his tongue loosed, and he spoke, blessing God. 65 And fear came on all their neighbors. And all these things were talked about through all the hill country of Judea, 66 and all who heard them laid them up in their hearts, saying, "What then will this child be?" For the hand of the Lord was with him.

67 And his father Zechariah was filled with the Holy Spirit and prophesied, saying,

68 "Blessed be the Lord God of Israel, for he has visited and redeemed his people… (You can look up and read the entire blessing in Luke 1:68-80)

Isn't it wonderful? The people who lost their blessing on the day of Atonement ended up with the greatest blessing of all nine months later. Zechariah's one appointed time to offer incense was immeasurably MORE than all he could have asked or imagined!

Now consider this . . . Zechariah, whose name means, *"Remember God,"* took the entire blessing home the day he was mute. He carried it to Elizabeth, whose name means *"Oath of God,"* and together they tell a story: *Remember God, Your oath.*

John's name means, *"The Lord is gracious"*

You might say their names together tell the story, **"God remembers His promise to be gracious."**

God remembers His promise to be gracious.

Digging Deeper

Looking back at the story, we find a large prayer gathering happening during the visit from the angel. Verse 10 tells us that "the whole multitude of the people were in prayer outside at the hour of the incense offering."

Gathering to seek God reflects two verses from the book of the prophet Jeremiah:

Look up Jeremiah 33:3 and write it out:

Write out Jeremiah 29:12 and 13a:

Considering the above verses, write your own prayer here:

Look again at Luke 1:9-10 and jot down the two things that were happening simultaneously:

Read the dialog between the angel Gabriel and Zechariah in Luke 1:12-20

Fear gripped Zechariah, and Gabriel reassured him with "Do not be afraid, your prayer has been heard . . . you will bear a son and name him John." Several promises were then issued.

How does Zechariah respond in verse 18?

What is the main result of his questioning the promise? (verse 20)

Now read Luke 1:21

So, God bound Zechariah's tongue. Jewish tradition kept the praying people waiting for the priest to return from offering incense in order to receive the blessing He was to speak over them.

No voice, no blessing . . . until nine months later.

- **Have you experienced being disciplined by God and then He poured out even greater blessings through your life later? If so, explain:**

Look up and read Genesis 22:16-17 and Micah 7:18-20.

- **How does this relate to Zechariah's stunning prophecy in Luke 1:67-80?**

In our failures and disappointments,

we can look for better things to come.

God Will . . . Wow!

Zechariah had seemingly lost hope in ever experiencing his “AHA!” – little did he know over the course of his mundane days, that after so much time, a day would come where God would not only “shock” his socks off, but would bless him and his beloved Elizabeth with an honor beyond their wildest imagination!

Notice Zechariah’s unbelief didn’t thwart God’s plan for his life! Obviously he had faith at least the size of a mustard seed! This is a delightful and encouraging story for us as we consider that our prayers are powerful and effective as children of God no matter how small our faith may seem!
What if all of our barren places, as children of God, are leading to a greater work of God than we’ve ever imagined? Could it be true that He who is able to do immeasurably MORE than we ask or imagine is right now working in ways we cannot see?!

Are you living in expectancy for God to answer the cries of your heart in surprising ways? Let’s press into Him for every desire He places on our hearts and trust Him with the answer above and beyond what we can fathom!

Prayer Prompt

God’s gifts and His call are irrevocable.

While our faith pleases God, our faithlessness doesn’t hinder Him.

As recipients of God’s covenant love, we should expect our own “AHA!”.

In our lives, we all will have times of great faith and also times of unbelief . Think over your life so far, and write a prayer thanking God for His grace to be strong in the hard times. Ask him for His grace to forgive your unbelief in weak times.

Then, ask Him for a fresh word for you as you anticipate His Spirit speaking to you.

Let the morning bring me word of your unfailing love, for I have put my trust in you. Show me the way I should go, for

to you I entrust my life. Psalm 143:8 NIV

Behold, I am doing a new thing; now it springs forth, do you not perceive it? I will make a way in the wilderness and rivers in the desert. Isaiah 43:19

9

JESUS

broken to fill

And this is eternal life, that they know you, the only true God, and Jesus Christ whom you have sent. (3)

I am praying for them . . . All mine are yours, and yours are mine, and I am glorified in them. And I am no longer in the world, but they are in the world, and I am coming to you. Holy Father, keep them in your name, which you have given me, that they may be one, even as we are one. (9-11)

But now I am coming to you, and these things I speak in the world, that they may have my joy fulfilled in themselves. (13)

I in them and you in me, that they may become perfectly one, so that the world may know that you sent me and loved them even as you loved me. (23)

I made known to them your name, and I will continue to make it known, that the love with which you have loved me may be in them, and I in them. (26)

Jesus' final prayer found in John 17

Does Jesus Really Want To Fill Me With Joy?

I want you . . . and I want you to want Me.

This theme resounds throughout the Bible. It is the heart of the gospel message. We've seen Luke 11:13 several times throughout the course of this study. Jesus, encouraging us to persist in prayer, asks us a question, "If we who are evil give good gifts to our children, "*how much more will your Heavenly Father give the Holy Spirit to those who ask Him?"*

His abundance is mind-blowing! Lord, help us to grasp it! Help us to want You more!

In the August 6th entry of My Utmost For His Highest, Oswald Chambers writes, *"The point of prayer is not to get answers from God, but to have perfect and complete oneness with Him."* [1]

This is the crux of Jesus's final and fervent prayer to the Father before He was crucified. His passion is for our salvation. The Greek word for salvation is *"sozo"* which means wholeness or fullness. He is everything we will ever need.

God's abundance is mind-blowing!

I Can Access His Power

When I answered the phone, I heard my girlfriend's broken voice. She began to pour out her heart through tears, "*Kathy, I need you to pray."*

She inhaled deeply, struggling for words. *"We have seen her . . . behavior change . . . over the last two months, and with her failing to come home last night, we suspected something. . . Suddenly I heard God tell me to have Jana* (her name has changed to protect her privacy) take off her jacket. She was reluctant, but we insisted* . . . (more sobs) . . . *and . . . we found heroine tracks on her arms. We don't know what to do."*

1

Knowing there was only one thing to do, I pleaded with my friend in prayer, *"Father, we don't know what to do, but our eyes are on You. Nothing is impossible for You. Lead us. Make a way of deliverance."*

The next morning, I prayed the entire hour and a half it took me to get to my friend's house. We were going to take Jana to the hospital to be tested.

We were talking in the kitchen while waiting for Jana to get ready to go. In response to the shock we were expressing at his sister's rapid spiral into drug use, suddenly, eight year old Tanner quoted 1 Peter 5:8: *Be alert and of sober mind. Your enemy the devil prowls around like a roaring lion looking for someone to devour.*

Jana was an accomplished member of the swim team at her school. She had finished the season in March, and admitted, after her parent's discovery, to experimenting with lighter drugs about a year prior. The recreational drug usage had escalated from her first use of the prescription drug, oxycodone (street term: oxycontin) to heroin within a matter of two months.

Upon hearing Tanner's words, it felt as if God Himself had spoken. We were in the midst of a mighty spiritual battle, *and I knew many like it had already been won.*

I had recently celebrated another young lady's deliverance from alcohol addiction through Teen Challenge, an effective recovery program. Her mom and I had watched strongholds come down and hope be restored through Teen Challenge's ministry of the word of God. We knew healing also came through our fervent prayers.

I suggested the program for Jana.

After researching, they found the cost to be outside the realm of possibility for them.

We prayed again, that God would make a way. True to His word, He provided. Through gifts from family members, my friend's precious 15 year old daughter was admitted to the program. Over the course of the following year, I received many phone calls from my friend. Each time we went directly to our knees, pleading for His hand to set her free. Our countless prayers were answered. The joy our answered prayer has brought to this family is immeasurable.

It's been nine years since her graduation from the program, and Jana is a mature young woman, a joyful wife and mama who clings to the truth that set her free. At this writing, she is working for Teen Challenge in addiction prevention.

War was waged, promises claimed, prayers were raised, and God proved faithful. Not only was one heart restored, but a family was made whole. If one person is broken, the whole unit is affected. Jesus made this clear in a prayer at the end of His life on earth.

Jesus Loves

In John 17, Jesus has fulfilled his sandal-clad mission. He knows He is headed to the cross. After encouraging His disciples who are mourning the fact that He is leaving them,(John, chapters 14-16,) He simultaneously prays to the Father and offers a refrain of his heartening words with a glorious benediction within hearing range of His disciples.

Think about this: What would you want to do for your loved ones if you knew you were going to die? What would you make sure you told them?

You'd want to address the things necessary for the flourishing and safe keeping of your people when you are no longer with them.

Jesus knows where to go for provision and protection for His disciples. After His encouragement to them in the previous chapters, in John 17, He looks up to Heaven. He asks the Father to meet the needs that are of primary importance to Him. He is eager to secure God's glory, as well as sanctity, unity, and mission success for His followers.

He seeks provision inwardly, by way of sending His Spirit to keep us until our arrival on Heaven's shores, and physically for our needs to be met by God.

He also shines a spotlight on our love toward one another and his desire for the "complete unity" of His family.

Can you relate to desiring wholeness in your family?

Read John 17:1-5

> 1 When Jesus had spoken these words, he lifted up his eyes to heaven, and said, "Father, the hour has come; glorify your Son that the Son may glorify you,2 since you have given him authority over all flesh, to give eternal life to all whom you have given him. 3 And this is eternal life, that they know you, the only true God, and Jesus Christ whom you have sent. 4 I glorified you on earth, having accomplished the work that you gave me to do. 5 And now, Father, glorify me in your own presence with the glory that I had with you before the world existed.

Jesus lifted His eyes to the Father, and prayed, *"Father, The hour has come; glorify me that I may glorify You."* He continues this first section of his prayer by declaring His authority to grant eternal life to all whom His Father has given to Him. He closes it with a statement that seems to hold great anticipation as it reflects the beginning of His prayer with several more uses of the word "glory."

It's as if He is saying, *"I'M COMING HOME TO GLORY!!! . . . I've accomplished the task I was sent out to do: I've opened the way for our people to join us in glory, and now I am coming home!! I can't wait to put the glory back on!"*

Friends, Jesus knows how it feels to LONG for Home! He understands the groanings of our flesh for eternal glory. He feels our anticipation for the perfection of Heaven! This is the joy set before Him that enabled Him to endure the cross and despise it's shame! It is the same holy anticipation we are called to hold onto in order to endure the crosses we are appointed to carry while we live in the land of our sojourn.

Read 2 Corinthians 4:16-18

> So we do not lose heart. Though our outer self is wasting away, our inner self is being renewed day by day. For this light momentary affliction is preparing for us an eternal weight of glory beyond all comparison, as we look not to the things that are seen but to the things that are unseen. For the things that are seen are transient, but the things that are unseen are eternal.

This encouragement *"do not lose heart,"* is meant to strengthen us in every battle we face in the spiritual war this side of heaven.

Look at the things unseen. Only we who have been given the light of Christ can even understand that statement. We are people who walk by faith and not by sight. We are the people who live our lives banking on the promises of God being more true for us than what we see with our eyes, feel with our hearts, or experience in our lives. We are the people whose eyes are fixed on truth and eternal glory!

Our lives are meant to be lived in this one holy note of joy: *"I have been raised with Christ"* (Notice the past tense of Colossians 3:1-4)

Because of our new birth and the fact that Jesus has authority over all flesh, we are already seated in Him in Heaven. This is worth meditating on!

Read John 17:6-19

> 6 "I have manifested your name to the people whom you gave me out of the world. Yours they were, and you gave them to me, and they have kept your word. 7 Now they know that everything that you have given me is from you. 8 For I have given them the words that you gave me, and they have received them and have come to know in truth that I came from you; and they have believed that you sent me. 9 I am praying for them. I am not praying for the world but for those whom you have given me, for they are yours. 10 All mine are yours, and yours are mine, and I am glorified in them. 11 And I am no longer in the world, but they are in the world, and I am coming to you. Holy Father, keep them in your name, which you have given me, that they may be one, even as we are one. 12 While I was with them, I kept them in your name, which you have given me. I have guarded them, and not one of them has been lost except the son of destruction, that the Scripture might be fulfilled. 13 But now I am coming to you, and these things I speak in the world, that they may have my joy fulfilled in themselves. 14 I have given them your word, and the world has hated them because they are not of the world, just as I am not of the world. 15 I do not ask that you take them out of the world, but that you keep them from the evil one. 16 They are not of the world, just as I am not of the world.17 Sanctify them in the truth; your word is truth. 18 As you sent me into the world, so I have sent them into the world. 19 And for their sake I consecrate myself, that they also may be sanctified in truth.

Jesus makes it clear that the Father is the One who has given the disciples, including us, *to* Jesus. How glorious! We know that Jesus is a gift to us, but we don't often consider that *we are a gift given to Jesus* by the Father!

Every good and perfect gift comes from the Father. Even the authority of Jesus was given to Him by God. Jesus' humble obedience is evidence of this. He gladly submitted to the will of the Father, thus establishing the example we are to follow.

Jesus goes on to declare the Heavenly transactions that have been made through His ministry to His followers. His prayer expresses that the word of truth, which was given by the Father, has been received, believed, and kept by the disciples. He claims that those who believe and embrace Jesus as coming from the Father, will remain in the world to carry on His work.

Jesus continues, asking God the Father to keep us, make us one, maintain our distinction from the world, protect us from the evil one, and sanctify us by God's word of truth.

There's so much here. But for now let's hone in on one key verse:

Listen again to what Jesus said in John 17:13:

> *But now I am coming to you (Father,) and these things I speak in the world, so that they may have* ***my joy*** *<u>fulfilled</u> in themselves.*

Joy is such a tiny word, but it is the heart of Jesus' prayer. Jesus tucked it inside the middle of twenty six verses, following the words, *"so that"* -- pointing to *"fullness of joy"* as the very core of his desire for us.

Listen to Psalm 16:11:

> *You make known to me the path of life;*
> *in your presence there is <u>fullness</u> of* ***joy****;*
> *at your right hand are pleasures forevermore.*

The answer to Jesus' prayer came in Acts 2:1-4 when He sent His presence to dwell in us:

> *When the day of Pentecost arrived, they were <u>all together</u> in <u>one</u> place. And suddenly there came from heaven a*

> *sound like a mighty rushing wind, and it filled the entire house where they were sitting. And divided* ***tongues as of fire*** *appeared to them and rested on each one of them. And they were all filled with* ***the Holy Spirit*** *and began to speak in other tongues as the Spirit gave them utterance.*

Tongues of fire came down -- but no longer would consume man's offering, as had been the case in the Old Testament. Instead, the fire of God could "light" upon the redeemed -- without consuming them!! Because of the sacrifice of the Son, the blood He shed established our holiness. Therefore, the Holy Spirit could *be at home* within us who've become "living sacrifices!"

The Word was made flesh and dwelt among us . . . and upon rising from the grave, has made His home in our hearts. *Now, the word is being revealed through us.*

Do you suddenly see on a whole new level, the holy joy-eruption in the victory celebration of our King as He prays in John 17?

Oh, may we believe and experience His rich love and overflow with joyful songs!

After Jesus ascended into Heaven, He sent His Spirit to indwell the believers who were gathered together, praying and waiting. (Acts 1-2) We might wonder if the "new tongues" that overflowed from the lips of the disciples were, in that holy moment, indicative of the new heart that was holy and free to house the Holy Spirit. When He came in, the heart overflowed and the mouth spoke!!!

We may not speak in new tongues every time our joy in the Holy Spirit erupts, but it's highly likely we could burst into song . . . or clap and give a shout as our feet leave the ground!

It's as if they *had* to speak in a tongue other than their own to express something so new, so unique . . . they couldn't use words that they understood.

How do you express your joy in the Holy Spirit?

Our Father's one ambition -- this Holy mission to be united with us, *to fill us,* was accomplished by the obedience of Jesus.

God's union with us is the fulfillment of joy!

Read what author E.M. Bounds says about prayer:

> *"Prayer in its highest form of faith . . . carries the whole man as a sacrificial offering. Thus devoting the whole man himself, and his all, to God in a definite, intelligent vow, never to be broken, in a quenchless and impassioned desire for Heaven."* [2]

Oh come, Oh come, Immanuel . . . Thank you that you love us so fervently!

> *. . . How much more will your Heavenly Father give the HOLY SPIRIT to those who ask Him?* **Luke 11:13**

*Fill us with **JOY** in Your Presence, O LORD!*

Digging Deeper

Remember the vacancy of heart we talked about in Chapter three; the empty bucket, symbolic of the absence of the God in our unregenerate souls?

The God-given needs we listed for love and acceptance, significance and security, care and empathy, creative expression, rest, freedom, domain & leadership, justice, and worship of our God, are all fulfilled in our restored relationship with God the Father through Jesus, by the work of the Holy Spirit.

Consider:

- **If you were fulfilled in each of these areas, would you feel fully joyful?**

- **Is it realistic to feel full joy while we live in the flesh?**

2

- **How is it possible to maintain joy before we reach Heaven, even in dark times?**

Read 2 Corinthians 6:10; 8:2 and write down any further thoughts about our human experience as Heavenly children living in the flesh.

Read Isaiah 53:3 and Hebrews 12:2

- **Together, these verses show Jesus lived the same dichotomy we do as believers. A life of blended sorrow and joy. How does this encourage you?**

Read Romans 5:1-5 and paraphrase:

May the God of hope fill you with all joy and peace in believing, so that by the power of the Holy Spirit you may abound in hope.
Romans 15:13

Jesus Is Our Joy

It is our certain hope in the Gospel of Jesus Christ, and in the power of the Holy Spirit dwelling in us that enables us to maintain our joy in future glory. Even in the midst of dark circumstances, we have the assurance of His keeping presence.

It is hard for us to imagine the suffering of believers throughout history. We might wonder if we could ever endure being burned on a stake as William Tyndale was, or face being beheaded like so many Christians already have.

Rather than wonder at our ability to endure, we can marvel at God's grace that keeps every believer safe even if we lose our lives -- because we have already been raised with Christ and are seated with Him in Heaven. Let the whole future rest in His hands!

Just as Jesus prayed at the end of His earthly ministry, scripture assures us that He always lives to intercede for us today. He is our great High Priest in Heaven who is seeing to our safe arrival. Just as He prayed for His followers, we should pray for those who are following us in faith. He promises our prayers will be answered and we will have fullness of joy. (John 16:24b)

The essence of God's love is JOY.

Our union with Christ in God -- is Glory.

Our JOY is fully fulfilled in our union with Jesus.

Prayer Prompt

Today, spend time praising Jesus for His prayers for you, and for giving you His Spirit. Listen for His voice, and write His words to you.

Consequently, he is able to save to the uttermost those who draw near to God through him, since he always lives to make intercession for them. Hebrews 7:25

Likewise the Spirit helps us in our weakness. For we do not know what to pray for as we ought, but the Spirit himself intercedes for us with groanings too deep for words.
Romans 8:26

10

MARY

favored & blessed

"Sing, O childless woman,
you who have never given birth!
Break into loud and joyful song, O Jerusalem,
you who have never been in labor.
For the desolate woman now has more children
than the woman who lives with her husband,"
says the Lord.
"Enlarge your house; build an addition.
Spread out your home, and spare no expense!
For you will soon be bursting at the seams.
Your descendants will occupy other nations
and resettle the ruined cities.
Isaiah 54:1-3 NLT

And Mary said, "Behold, I am the servant of the Lord;
let it be to me according to your word.
Luke 1:38

And Elizabeth was filled with the Holy Spirit, and she
exclaimed with a loud cry, "Blessed are you among women,
and blessed is the fruit of your womb!
Luke 1:41-42

How Does God See Women?

As women who like to gather and grow together to glean spiritual fortitude, build bonds of love, and increase our fervor for the mission of God, closing a study on prayer by focusing on the mother of Jesus seems fitting.

We are women. We are fruit-bearers.

We are mothers.

As daughters of God, many of us will bear fruit through our womb, and some will not. But because we are born of the Spirit, all of us are bearing fruit for the Kingdom through spiritual child-bearing. Women are all meant to be mothers, spiritually speaking.

Jesus made this declaration one day by saying to a woman in the crowd who, upon seeing His power and glory, raised her voice and said to him,

> *"Blessed is the womb that bore you,*
> *and the breasts at which you nursed!"*
> *But he said, "Blessed rather are those*
> *who hear the word of God and keep it!"*
> **Luke 11:27-28**

I Am A Mother

My mom nurtured twelve children in her womb and nursed them all at her breast. She said, "yes" to her body being a home twelve times.

I was often by her side as she studied, led Bible studies, and prayed during my teen years. My life's work reflects her heart for God's word.

In relation to your own fruitfulness in the Kingdom of God, if you receive even one nugget of encouragement to draw near to God and increase your fervency in prayer from going through this study, you have, in small part, my mom to thank. Jesus of course is the source, but He will credit faithful service to my mom, as well as to you and the many people who you fellowship with today.

Additionally, if many of you pray for God's ministries on a regular basis, each woman who receives 'even a cold cup of water' from the refreshing word of God through the work of that ministry is supplying a crown you will one day lay at the feet of Jesus.

What are the crowns we will lay at the feet of Jesus? Revelation 4:10 describes the elders casting their crowns before the throne. As the redeemed of the Lord, and as servants of our God, we too will cast our crowns.

The crowns signify the victories won through the authority delegated to us by Jesus. Ephesians 2:10 tells us that God has created good works for each of us to do while we are here. As we walk intimately with Jesus, and as we take the steps of faith and obedience He calls us to, we will bear fruit and we will receive crowns.

Consider the words of the Apostle Paul as he tells the Philippians, believers in Jesus through the ministry of Paul, to imitate him and to pay careful attention to those who live according to the example seen in their teachers and elders. After reminding them that they are citizens of Heaven who await their Savior, he says, "*Therefore, my brothers, whom I love and long for, my joy and crown, stand firm thus in the Lord, my beloved.*" (Philippians 4:1)[1]

Paul's love and service to the Philippians meant that he was a spiritual father to them. He describes his "spiritual children" as his "joy and crown."

My daughter recently published a poem on Instagram. As I read it, it sounded very similar to one I would write. I don't know if I'd ever read a poem she'd written, so when I saw her name at the end, I was delighted because I recognized myself in her words. She is my crown!

As parents of adults, and as grandparents, I doubt there is anything that brings my husband and I more joy than to see those coming after us reflect the qualities we've invested in them. We also enjoy talking about the inherent characteristics God placed within them

1

such as our son's ability to rebuild car engines, reflecting his father, and our daughter's ability to pen a poem, reflecting my own penchant for prose. No doubt you can relate from your own observations of children.

Ultimately, as children of God, we are His crown. Surely that is what he meant upon His creation of Adam and Eve, as He described those He kissed with His breath, *the image-bearing segment* of His creation with the words, *"it was very good"* -- after having said of His other magnificent works, simply, *"it was good."*

All credit for our fruitfulness in Kingdom work is due to the wisdom and power of the Life Giver. When He lives within us, He gives us everything we need for doing His will. This is the reason for casting our crowns. These crowns are His to begin with, and we are humbled by the honor of having them bestowed on us.

This is worship.

Jesus In Us

Let your heart grab hold of this fact: *our salvation is hinged on Mary's "Yes" to God.*

Read Luke 1:38

> 38 And Mary said, "Behold, I am the servant of the Lord; let it be to me according to your word." And the angel departed from her.

The conversation begins with a greeting from the angel Gabriel: *"Greetings Favored woman . . ."* and he continues to relay God's message to Mary, who is at least a tiny bit scared.

Mary responds to the announcement that she will get pregnant, at first with a question. *"How can it be that I'd be with child since I am a virgin?"*

Gabriel explains to her that the Holy Spirit will come upon her and the Most High will overshadow her. Basically, he tells Mary that God is going to be the Father of the child she is to call Jesus.

Her words, *"I am the Lord's servant, may it be done to me according to your word."* display the prayer that believes and receives the Word of the Lord.

Mary's answer was essentially, "Yes, Lord."

Read Luke 1:39-40

> 39 In those days Mary arose and went with haste into the hill country, to a town in Judah, 40 and she entered the house of Zechariah and greeted Elizabeth.

In his conversation with Mary, the angel, Gabriel had pointed to Elizabeth as an example of the miracle-working power of God over a womb. It seems there was more to the "point" of Gabriel's pointing, as Mary *hastens* to travel to spend time with Elizabeth.

How well God knows His creatures! What woman wouldn't want to go as soon as possible to confirm such news! It's a mighty force, the magnetic pull on our female hearts, when we hear the words, *"You too?!"*

Mary "hustled" to visit one who would "get her" in this non-conventional calling to carry God's Son.

Read Luke 1:41-45

> 41 And when Elizabeth heard the greeting of Mary, the baby leaped in her womb. And Elizabeth was filled with the Holy Spirit, 42 and she exclaimed with a loud cry, "Blessed are you among women, and blessed is the fruit of your womb! 43 And why is this granted to me that the mother of my Lord should come to me? 44 For behold, when the sound of your greeting came to my ears, the baby in my womb leaped for joy. 45 And blessed is she who believed that there would be a fulfillment of what was spoken to her from the Lord."

There is only one explanation for the eruption of joy within Elizabeth's womb, or for the gleeful proclamation that came from her lips. It is none other than the Presence of the Holy Spirit.

Think of it! How your own heart does a little dance when you are together with other sisters celebrating a victory, and answered prayer, or discovering the depths of the riches of God in His word!

Without a doubt, the happy greeting served Mary every ounce of confirmation she needed to never waver for a moment, to never fall into thinking she'd only been dreaming when she was visited by Gabriel.

God said it, she believed it, and He gave her confirmation enough to keep believing.

If we have discovered anything in these ten weeks of study on prayer, it is the often overwhelming ecstasy that erupts from our union with the Lord through His Holy Spirit. We cannot miss that it always revolves around conversations with the Divine, and the reception of His Holy word to us personally.

Immediately following Elizabeth's glorious proclamation over Mary,
"Blessed is she who has believed that the Lord will fulfill what he has spoken to her!"

Mary spills her own joy, by way of a song.

Luke 1:46-55

"My soul magnifies the Lord,
and my spirit rejoices in God my Savior,
for he has looked on the humble estate of his servant.
For behold, from now on all generations will call me blessed;
for he who is mighty has done great things for me,
and holy is his name.
And his mercy is for those who fear him
from generation to generation.
He has shown strength with his arm;
he has scattered the proud in the thoughts of their hearts;
he has brought down the mighty from their thrones
and exalted those of humble estate;
he has filled the hungry with good things,
and the rich he has sent away empty.
He has helped his servant Israel,
in remembrance of his mercy,
as he spoke to our fathers,
to Abraham and to his offspring forever."

Jesus left glory and came down to be nurtured in Mary's womb, and to be nourished at her breasts... *so that* (remember this clause from our study of Jesus' prayer, having joy as its aim?) He could return to GLORY and come back down to dwell in us. He would not dwell in our wombs that carry earthly life, but in our hearts that carry eternal life -- by faith.

Our hearts are tabernacles for Jesus' *glorified* presence.

Jesus presence in us is our fullness of joy!

Let's get a glimpse of the glory of our risen Savior.
Read Revelation 1:12-18:

> 12 Then I turned to see the voice that was speaking to me, and on turning I saw seven golden lampstands, 13 and in the midst of the lampstands one like a son of man, clothed with a long robe and with a golden sash around his chest. 14 The hairs of his head were white, like white wool, like snow. His eyes were like a flame of fire. 15 his feet were like burnished bronze, refined in a furnace, and his voice was like the roar of many waters. 16 In his right hand he held seven stars, from his mouth came a sharp two-edged sword, and his face was like the sun shining in full strength.
> 17 When I saw him, I fell at his feet as though dead. But he laid his right hand on me, saying, "Fear not, I am the first and the last, 18 and the living one. I died, and behold I am alive forevermore, and I have the keys of Death and Hades.

John, the same one who wrote the gospel, the same one who labeled himself "the disciple Jesus loved" -- upon seeing the glorified Christ, *fell at his feet as dead.*

Whomp!

Before the death, burial, and resurrection of Jesus, the glorious Presence could have killed John. Instead, what happened? King Jesus touched him, and then gave him a task. *"Write, therefore, the things you have seen . . ." (v19)*

Now, it is the glorified King of Heaven who nourishes and nurses us from within. He fills us with His eternal life, and with His word *so that* He can be displayed through our lives to the world who does not yet know Him. What has He commissioned you to do?

If you've ever seen a bridegroom beam, imagine the same look on Jesus' face when your own hand holds firm to his elbow on your way down the aisle toward Heaven.

Many people might love to study Jesus' words, might love the idea of Jesus, love His works, his compassion, his kindness . . . but do not truly know Him . . . and do not truly love Him.

How do we know that we love Him? By obeying His commands.
Not from duty, but from delight.
Not by human effort, but by His Spirit.

This is why 1 John 5:3 says His commands are not burdensome. Because our obedience is not by way of our effort, but through our surrender to His Lordship. Through yielding our will to the authority of God, our Father, we are made holy.

The world will know we are Christians by our love and by our unity. God knows, and we know that we love Him, by our submission and obedience to His word.

To submit and obey requires ongoing dialogue (prayer) between:
Father and daughter.
Brother and sister.
Friend to friend.

Prayer is the intercorse (dialogue) between God and His people.
Prayer is a divine conversation.
Prayer is the union which produces lasting, eternal fruit.

It seems like the prayer Jesus prayed
at the close of His days on Earth,
might be the bridge between Mary's song and yours . . .

> *"Now I am coming to you, (Father). I told them many things while I was with them in this world so they would be **filled with my joy. I have given them your word.***

. . . They do not belong to this world any more than I do. Make them holy by your truth; teach them your word, which is truth. Just as you sent me into the world, I am sending them into the world. And I give myself as a holy sacrifice for them so they can be made holy by your truth.

. . . Father, I want these whom you have given me to be with me where I am. Then they can see all the glory you gave me because you loved me even before the world began! "O righteous Father, the world doesn't know you, but I do; and these disciples know you sent me. I have revealed you to them, and I will continue to do so. ***Then your love for me will be in them, and I will be in them."***

John 17:13-20,24-26 NLT[2]

Digging Deeper

- **Read John 13:35 - How will the world know we are Christians?**

- **Read John 17:23 - How will the world know we are Christians?**

- **Read Matthew 7:15-20 - How do believers recognize false teachers?**

- **Read Matthew 7:21-23 - Can people do amazing things that seem good, but have no eternal life in them?**

2

- **Read 1 John 5:3 - How do we show our love for God?**

- **Ephesians 1:13 - What ultimately keeps us in Jesus? *(See also: Hebrews 10:23, 3:14, 4:14)***

Hopefully, your answer to the last question was by way of our new birth, having the Spirit of God within us enabling us to keep his commandments.

If you are in Christ, but not experiencing the fruits of the Spirit -- it simply means you've got to surrender something more to His Lordship.

Do you lack any of these? (and we all do) . . . love, joy, peace, patience, kindness, gentleness, faithfulness, goodness, or self-control?

Perhaps you are still holding on to control, or to having your way. Perhaps you focus on yourself or on your problem more than on Jesus and His promises.

- **Ask Jesus what He wants to reveal to you, and how He wants you to surrender.**

When we sense these things are absent, we can be encouraged as born-again believers, to go to the Lord and seek the fruit of the Holy Spirit. Remember, there is no condemnation for those who are in Christ Jesus! (Romans 8:1) Our failures should always have us returning to the cross where we receive forgiveness, and then on to the throne of grace to receive mercy and help for our need.

Read Luke 1:54-55 in Mary's song.

Her words reveal that Mary knew scripture, and she knew the promises of God. Her heart longed for His glory. Her knowledge of God, and her love for His word, were foundational to her believing and receiving the Word of the Lord.

- **How can you become more familiar with God's word and His promises?**

- **What will you do to increase your prayer life?**

May we be women who
believe and receive the Word of the Lord.

May we be women who
love God's word and trust His promises.

May we be women who
constantly converse with the Divine.

My Yes To God

Just as Mary's "Yes!" to God meant salvation came to us, our "Yes!" to God means salvation will come through us. Life always begets life. This is the way of our God, eternal multiplication.

He spoke the world into existence by His word. He brings transformation and new life in the same way. Our faith comes by hearing and our hearing by the Word of God. The Word took on flesh and dwelt among us, now He is revealing the word through our surrendered flesh.

One essential fruit of our salvation that is not listed with the others, but implied all through scripture, is our love for God's glory. Our one desire for Him will cause us to despise anything that would come between us and our King.

This is the fruit of the Spirit that, when paired with faith in His mercy, leads to our hot pursuit of our King, our zeal to contend for the truth that sanctifies, and our willingness to surrender all to His Lordship. Prayer is the fuel for all of it.

Just as Jesus obeyed everything His Father commanded him to do and accomplished His mission, we too will be fruitful in the land of the living through our communion with God. We are among those highly favored and blessed by God, who gather with Him.

Prayer Prompt

Read the words from the gospel of Luke that Mary heard as if they are to you, and then scribe your own song to God using the words of Mary to lead yours . . .

> "Greetings, O favored one, the Lord is with you!" Luke 1:28
>
> "Behold, I am the servant of the Lord; let it be to me according to your word."
> Luke 1:38
>
> "My soul magnifies the Lord,
> and my spirit rejoices in God my Savior,
> for he has . . .

"Blessed is she who has believed that the Lord would fulfill his promises to her!"
Luke 1:45

Favored & Blessed

Jesus

We see

The way You came.

The love You give,

We bear Your name.

You bought us back,

You made a way,

For us

To live

Forever

Today

Full of joy

Peace and power,

You're the gift

We need each hour.

You are faithful

To intercede

You provide

Our every need.

We thank you,

Lord,

Your grace is great

Your victory, sure

Our hope, secure.

Lord, may I Believe & Receive and hold fast to your word to me, as Abraham did.

May it be true that I Wrestled into You & have been Revived by you, as Jacob was.

Make my heart be Fervent & Overflowing with faith and love for You, like Hannah's.

Grant me grace to Surrender & live my life as an minister of Salvation, as Jonah did.

May I be known as one who Intercedes & Advances your mission, as Moses did.

May my work for your house be Zealous & may I be found Faithful, as Nehemiah was.

May my life exhibit Your Power & Presence, bringing You Pleasure, as Solomon did.

I will seek Your "AHA!" answers to prayer & pour out praise to You, as Zechariah did.

I will surrender my life to be Broken with You that many may be filled with Your joy.

Thank you that I am a woman like Mary, Favored & Blessed to bear You, my Savior!

May I shine bright for you.

In the name of Jesus, amen!

Please tuck this book in a place where you can return to read your penned prayers in the years to come.

Perhaps every new year, you could return to it, and watch the progress that the Lord makes in your faith.

Recording your prayers and praises is extremely valuable for your faith, and of those who come behind you.

GROUP

discussion questions

1 ABRAHAM believes & receives

Have you found yourself "face down" in the carpet due to something way beyond your control, power, or abilities?

1. **When has desperation driven you to your knees?**
2. **Name your greatest fear.**
3. **Tell about a time when you received beautiful 'resurrection' life out of a place of dust and ashes.**
4. **What has God called you to leave behind that felt costly?**
5. **Share something from your life that God has uprooted, something that once bound you that you are free of?**
6. **When you were born again into the family of God, like AbrAHam and SarAH, you received a new identity. Do you live with greater awareness of your eternal identity than that of your earthly one?** (Does your life reflect one of valuing and caring for your soul more than your physical appearance and circumstances? Do you focus on eternity more than your temporal life?)
7. **Do you picture God as one who enjoys laughter or is this a surprise to you? (Expand)**
8. **Share about a time when you laughed with God.**
9. **What is it you're currently seeking from God that you are certain aligns with His character and His will that we can pray together for?**
10. **Share a promise from scripture that God has given to you personally to pray.**

Chapter two and three will deal with our weaknesses. The goal of these sections is for God to cement the truth that we are recipients of grace, and His mercy will not fail us. As daughters of the King, we don't ever need to be afraid of being open and honest about our struggles.

What we bring into the Light will be healed.

1. **What fears emerged during your childhood that you found ways to compensate for without God, and continue to default to as an adult?**

2. **Name the methods of self-preservation or self-justification you are prone to relying on instead of resting in Jesus' love for you.** (For example: lying, seeking validation from peers, dominating, medicating, giving up, staying home, arguing, blaming, etc.)

3. **"Stew" (Instant gratification) clouded both Esau and his father Isaac's judgement. Are there things in your life, handed down through your family line that might cause you to be "blind" -- weak areas or blind spots where the enemy might steal from you?** (For example: materialism, alcoholism, unforgiveness, anger, impatience, etc)

4. **Jacob entered into a wilderness where he was refined through his experiences. God uprooted the error of his ways and revealed his need for God's faithfulness. You might be in a wilderness time in your life right now, wondering if the cloud will ever lift or the new day will come.**

    - **Does Jacob's story serve as encouragement to trust God in your sorrow, pain, or loss?**

    - **Do you believe that all of your difficult trials are God's loving hand upon your life, since you are His chosen and beloved daughter?**

5. **What have you wrestled in prayer for that brought you greater intimacy with God?**

6. **Both Jacob (Israel) and Simon (Peter) received a new name as a result of intimacy with God. Can you name one way that God has changed you?** (For example: From "Striving to Surrender" or From "Deceptive to Trusting")

Talk through the list below of God-given needs, being gentle and gracious with one another. Remember these are things we progress in on our journey with Jesus, and we will only be complete in Heaven.

- Love and Acceptance: Do you feel a sense of belonging within the Family of God? Are you offering love and acceptance to others?

- Significance and Security: Do you feel significant to God and secure in His love? Are you seeking to offer others a sense of significance and security?

- Care and Empathy: Do you feel cherished and cared for by God and His people? Are you caring for others and empathizing with their sorrows and struggles?

- Creative expression: As an image-bearer of our Creator, how are you reflecting Him as a creative -- through your unique sets of gifts or your role in your relationships?

- Rest: He gave us a desire and need for peace, ease, harmony, and absence of tension. Do you, by faith, make room for a regular rhythm of rest in your schedule?

- Freedom: Do you enjoy freedom in Christ, not bound by perfectionism or striving to please people? Do you allow others freedom to do things differently from you?

- Dominion and Leadership: Do you walk by faith in the places of leadership God has called you to, trusting Him as your source of wisdom, strength, and provision?

- Justice: Do you believe your seat at God's table is equal in every way to others, or do you struggle with feeling as if you've been short-changed, being trapped in a spirit of comparison?

- Worship: Do you find your eyes more on God than on yourself or others?

As we studied the life of Hannah, we saw that she exhibited endurance and longsuffering, with her heart perpetually turned toward the Lord. She appears to have understood the fact that if there was a void in her life, it was God alone who could fill it. She pressed in, prayerfully, to apprehend the desire of her soul, and because of her faith, she received what her heart truly longed for.

Pray for one another, that the Lord will increase faith, hope, and love in your hearts by the power of the Holy Spirit.

Is there an event in your life where you were given an abundance of grace? Do you have a story of gritty faith...one with no other explanation than the Spirit of God took over your heart, giving you strength to endure victoriously?

- **If so, how did the Lord sustain you?**
- **Have you had the opportunity to comfort others with the comfort you received from Him?**

Or, have you ever run away from God's call on your life due to fear or stubbornness?

- **If so, how did He bring you back?**
- **How did your disobedience affect others around you?**
- **How has He brought good out of that time in your life?**

When we've been baptized into Christ's death, our soul will never die, but our fear, disobedience, and unbelief will bring a type of death-- a death to our own way, or rather, a death to our flesh. When this happens, we are refined, and God uses our desolate places to bring life. There was a point of decision in Jonah's life, when the finger of God pointed at him, giving him opportunity to own up to his sin. Sometimes God will allow Satan, the "accuser" to point his finger at our failings* -- not to shame us, but to give us opportunity to agree with our adversary, repent, and receive God's free and amazing grace. This is our blood-bought freedom. (*You must always weigh any guilt you feel against what is real. The enemy will falsely accuse you also, but this also serves God's purposes to train you to discern. God's word is our source of discerning His voice. Our accurate assessment of our lives - "is this true?" - is also necessary. If in doubt, ask a friend to help you.)

- **Share what it is like to have experienced this kind of freedom upon receiving God's mercy.**

- **How has God used your freedom to help someone else get free?**

Next time God allows your "boat" to experience a storm, what will you remember from the stories of Jonah and of the disciples in the storm with Jesus asleep in the boat?

Close by praying for anyone who is experiencing a storm.

- **Would someone be willing to share a story of a time when prayer brought dramatic transformation to circumstances?**

- **Moses's mother knew God's hand was upon her son. How have you experienced the hand of God upon your life? If you are a mom, how have you seen it upon your children?**

Doing God's work man's way led Moses into the wilderness. We see evidence of the demise of doing things man's way all around us. Prisons are at max capacity. The media is full of mocking voices and critical spirits.

- **How can we guard our hearts against getting caught up in the ways of the world?**

At the end of Moses' wilderness experience, he encounters God in the burning bush.

- **Where have you encountered God?**

When God is angry and wants to destroy the Israelites, He talks to Moses and makes it sound like the Israelites are Moses's children. Imagine the weight Moses could have taken on at the time -- it would have crushed him. Instead, he interceded, praying for God's will and God's glory, thus acting as intercessor.

- **When have you transferred a weight off of your shoulders onto God's and seen deliverance?**

Moses, Paul, and Job were so attentive and in tune to the charge God had given them as leaders/parents that their prayers were intentional and intense. This kept them dependent on God rather than manipulative or fearful for those in their care. It also kept them close to God.

Intercession connects you to God and connects your people to God. It also enables us to keep the bigger picture in mind -- remembering that God is God and you are not.

- **Spend some time together praying for one another for your leadership roles.**

Zeal is defined as, *"Fervor in advancing a cause or rendering service."* In scripture, it can also mean *"God's jealous concern for His people or their welfare."* The word "passionate" can be synonymous with the word zealous.

- **What are you most zealous for?**

- **Have you sensed a specific calling on your life? If so, share what it is. If not, you may be currently living it or He may not yet have revealed it. (God calls us to move on to different things as we walk with Him.)**

- **What comes to mind when you read the following quote?**
  "Your deepest desires fuel your prayers."

- **What deep desires and longings move you regularly to prayer?**

  - **As people share their heart's dreams and longings, encourage one another by affirming what you've observed in each other's lives.** (For example: If someone wants to minister to freed human trafficking survivors, God will place certain gifts in the person with that dream -- you can recognize that and confirm those gifts in them.)

- **Considering Nehemiah's story . . . There is clear evidence that God had prepared Nehemiah for the day His hand would begin setting things in motion. Much of our lives are preparation for the next thing God is doing. Preparation means we are waiting.**

  - **Talk about what helps you keep your eyes on God while you wait for the things you are longing for.**

- **When Jesus turned the tables in the entrance to the temple, He was showing His zeal for God's house, and the reason for His fervor was his desire for His Father's house to be a house of prayer. His goal has always been** intimacy with God. His passion is for union between God and His people.

  - Do the things you are zealous for fit into this category of reconciliation between God and man?

- Help one another see how God can use your dreams to make Himself known, and pray for the women in your small group.

The sacrifice of the wicked is an abomination to the Lord,
but the prayer of the upright is his delight.
Proverbs 15:8

As women in earthly bodies, living in a culture of individualism with social structures in place that can cause us to sort of sleep our way through life, we want to be counter-cultural. Our goal is to become gritty, faith-filled women of prayer.

- **What different positions do people take when they pray?**
- **Do you assume different positions at different times?**
- **Why might we benefit from different positions while we pray?**

In all of our day-to-day doings, in our mundane Monday moments, and in our freaky Friday fodder, God is just a prayer away. As born-again believers in Jesus, who've been given the Spirit of God to dwell inside of us, our bodies are the New Covenant Temple. Heaven is as close to us while we are folding laundry as it is when we are gathered in sacred assemblies.

- **Share times you are prone to pray in your day that are outside of your routine prayer time so you can spur one another on with ideas.**
- **Has God shown up in your life in a dramatic way, and nearly knocked you down with wonder?**
- **Where do you tend to experience a greater awareness of God's presence?**
- **When Solomon prays, "heal and forgive" three times, it implies the importance of the need for peace in our relationship with God.**
    - **Do you make repentance a regular part of your time in prayer; do you keep short accounts with God?**

    - **Do you receive His promise of cleansing and renewal?**

- **How is your heart stirred for prayer during this Bible study so far?**
- **What is the importance of being meeting with other believers for corporate prayer?**
- **Pray together.**

We've talked a lot about our hopes and dreams, our desires and longings. We've been astonished, along with God's people, by His amazing goodness, by His presence showing up, and at His amazing gift of grace, Immanuel.

Just think! In one glorious moment, everything can change because God moves!

- **How have you seen Him change things in answer to your prayers over the past seven weeks?**

God wants us to be people whose faces are turned toward Him with anticipation and expectancy. Zechariah's failure, and God's grace towards him, is encouraging. It shows us that we don't have to do this life perfectly in order for God to blow fresh wind through our lives. However, He'd love it if we responded in faith instead of unbelief. He wants us to be expectant children.

- **Let's go over these passages of scripture today. Read each of them out loud, and then pray for one another to live with expectancy for God to hear and answer our prayers.**

Whatever you ask in my name, this I will do, that the Father may be glorified in the Son.
John 14:13

If you abide in me, and my words abide in you, ask whatever you wish, and it will be done for you. John 15:7

You did not choose me, but I chose you and appointed you that you should go and bear fruit and that your fruit should abide, so that whatever you ask the Father in my name, he may give it to you. John 15:16

In that day you will ask nothing of me. Truly, truly, I say to you, whatever you ask of the Father in my name, he will give it to you.
John 16:23

- **Share any questions you have regarding these promises, and encourage one another.**

- **Look back at your Digging Deeper and comment on Jeremiah 33:3 and Jeremiah 29:12-13a**

- **Do you open your Bibles with anticipation of hearing God revealing secrets to you?**

- **Pray for one another to have ears to hear the Lord speak and believe what He says.**

If we were to summarize Jesus's prayer in John 17, we might say His prayer is for us to live full of joy in His "invisible Kingdom" while we live on earth. He had previously told the disciples, *"In this world you will have trouble, but take heart, I have overcome the world."*

Jesus has overcome the world we live in. He said from the cross, *"It is finished."*

It is a daily battle for us to walk by faith and not by sight. We cannot do the Christian life alone, and we cannot do it half-heartedly. We are told to be self-controlled and alert. We are encouraged to trust in the Lord with our whole heart.

1. **What stood out to you as you studied Jesus' fervent prayer for us this week?**

It's as if Jesus was on the end of a high diving board when He prayed this prayer in John 17, ready to take the plunge into the deep dark where no one wants to go, knowing He would come back up in resurrection power -- and that power would restore all things to all who place their faith in Him.

2. **Are you living aware of the spiritual battle that Jesus refers to when He asks the Father to protect us from the evil one?**

3. **Jesus' prayer for us gives us assurance of victory as we fight the spiritual battle on earth. Have you been able to grab hold of the assurance?**

4. **2 Cor 4:16-18 exhorts us to "fix our eyes on the things unseen" -- can you give practical examples of how to keep our eyes on eternity?**
    a. **When you look in the mirror . . . When you listen to the news . . . When you see your friend's Hawaiian vacation photos?**

    b. **Can you think of other scenarios where you need to shift your focus?**

"We don't often consider that *we are a gift given to Jesus* by the Father!"

5. **Respond to the fact that we are gifts to Jesus. How does it make you feel?**

6. **Have you experienced a time with amped up joy in the presence of God? Describe how you felt and responded.**

7. **Have you been able to embrace and hold the tension we live in -- that of sorrow and joy, in light of Jesus having endured the same thing while He lived here? Expand.** (Have you experienced His joy amidst a time of sorrow and loss?)

8. **Pray for one another.**

As women gather together to glean spiritual fortitude, build bonds of love, and increase our fervor for the mission of God -- closing a study on prayer by focusing on the mother of Jesus seems fitting.

We are women. We are fruit-bearers. We are mothers.

"Blessed is the womb that bore you, and the breasts at which you nursed!"
But he [Jesus] said, "Blessed rather are those who hear the word of God and keep it!"
Luke 11:27-28

1. **What do you think Jesus meant by His words?**
2. **Who has invested in your life spiritually through ministry of the Word, prayer, and encouragement?**
3. **Name qualities in your life that resemble those of your spiritual mentors?**
4. **Currently, who are you investing in spiritually?**
    a. **How often do you open the Word of God with them?**
    b. **What are your goals as you sow into their lives?**
5. **God provided a "mentor" for Mary in Elizabeth. He provided comfort and confirmation. How has He provided those things for you?**
6. **What would you title the song you would sing to God for His goodness to you?**
7. **By clinging to God's Word, we can live out His love and be united with His people, and He will shine through us. How much of a priority should we give to His Word in our lives? In our homes?**
8. **Dear sister, what might *your* "yes" to God mean for the world? Dream of it!**

Close by praying for each other.

Please tuck this book in a place where you can return to read your penned prayers in the years to come. Perhaps every new year, you could return to it, and watch the progress that the Lord makes in your faith. Recording your prayers and praises is extremely valuable for your faith, and of those who come behind you.

Praise and Thank our God often in the presence of your people. He will bless the fruit of your lips.

RESOURCES

to enhance study

Since music and books minister to me, I wanted to share suggested resources for you to expand your meditation on the truths in this study. I love to put a song on repeat when it holds an encouraging truth because I've experienced the Holy Spirit bring the lyrics back at "just the right time" so often.

I do pray your heart is tethered more tightly to Christ through digging into the conversations He has with His people in scripture. And I pray that your own conversations with Him will be increasingly fervent and fruitful.

Love,

Kathy Schwanke

Week One: Believes & Receives

Songs:
"Everything is Mine In You" by Christy Nockels
https://www.youtube.com/watch?v=zokDEfvD5gY

"You Are My One Thing" by Bethel Music
https://www.youtube.com/watch?v=lHptBGS_tAo

Find the meaning of your name:
http://www.top-100-baby-names-search.com/christian-meaning-of-names.html

Thoughts on God laughing by Liz Curtis Higgs:
http://www.lizcurtishiggs.com/does-god-laugh-out-loud/

Week Two: Wrestled & Revived

Songs:
"My Portion And My Strength" by Ellie Holcomb
https://www.youtube.com/watch?v=fXARDdmMs9Q

"The Unmaking" by Nicole Nordeman
https://www.youtube.com/watch?v=VQkHD15J7Hl

"It is Well" by Kristine DiMarco (Bethel worship version)
https://www.youtube.com/watch?v=YNqo4Un2uZI

Digging Deeper on Jacob:
http://www.jesuswalk.com/jacob/1_deceiver.htm

Books:
Wrestling Prayer: A Passionate Communion With God by Eric Ludy

Week Three: Fervent & Overflowing

Songs:
"My Anchor" by Christy Nockels
https://www.youtube.com/watch?v=0NG_D19wru0

"Jesus, Rock of Ages" by Christy Nockels
https://www.youtube.com/watch?v=UrWndpI7NNE

"The Voice of Truth" by Casting Crowns
https://www.youtube.com/watch?v=KwsvqVmFV6Y

Books:
Scribbling In The Sand by Michael Card (Christ and Creativity)
A Million Little Ways by Emily P. Freeman (Uncover The Art You Were Made To Live)

Week Four: Surrender & Salvation

Songs:
"You'll Get Through This" by Martina McBride
https://www.youtube.com/watch?v=oaOc7R18e1g

"Gracefully Broken" by Matt Redman
https://www.youtube.com/watch?v=IJNR0lxbIP4

"I Will Praise You in This Storm" by Casting Crowns
https://www.youtube.com/watch?v=L5bLvVjJ4MA

Book:
Altar'd by Jennifer Kennedy Dean
Dealing With the Rejection and Praise of Man by Bob Sorge

Week Five: Intercedes & Advances

Songs:
"I Lift My Friend Up To You" by Casting Crowns
https://www.youtube.com/watch?v=Jsx1DIc5o4A

"So Will I" by Tori Kelly
https://www.youtube.com/watch?v=IuedrKMVbFk

Books:
Powerful Prayers for Supernatural Results by Mike Shreve
Deepening Your Conversations With God by Ben Patterson
(Some of the content of this study was inspired by these two books)

Week Six: Zealous & Faithful

Songs:
"In Christ Alone" by Owl City
https://www.youtube.com/watch?v=Ipl-rLRxOrs

"You Are My Shepherd" by Tricia Brock
https://www.youtube.com/watch?v=KAQuJNHwLLE

Books:
The Uncommon Woman by Susie Larson

Week Seven: Power & Presence & Pleasure

Songs:
"Abba" by Jonathan & Melissa Helser
https://www.youtube.com/watch?v=7sroPrjCoGY

"Touch The Sky" by Hillsong United
https://www.youtube.com/watch?v=J33cjSzUhsA

"Explode My Soul" by Melissa Hesler
https://youtu.be/rxEwubliYhA

Books:
Holiness, Truth, and the Presence of God by Francis Frangipane

Week Eight: "AHA!"

Songs:
"Light Up The Sky" by The Afters
https://www.youtube.com/watch?v=8LQH6UDi15s

"Daughters of the King" by Tricia Brock
https://www.youtube.com/watch?v=065gjBjfqSg

"The Altar And The Door" by Casting Crowns
https://www.youtube.com/watch?v=z07HrK9fCF0

Book:
Spirit Rising by Jim Cymbala

Week Nine: Broken to Fill

Songs:
"You are Beloved" by Jordan Feliz
https://www.youtube.com/watch?v=q117T7-XD_k

"Come Alive" by Lauren Daigle
https://www.youtube.com/watch?v=0P4YdXz3LAI

Broken For Love's Sake by Tricia Brock
https://www.youtube.com/watch?v=SUGDaGVKC1o

Books:
The Radical Cross by A. W. Tozer
Crazy Love by Francis Chan

Week Ten: Favored & Blessed

Songs:
"Ever Be" by Kalley Heiligenthal
https://www.youtube.com/watch?v=byEUIzfVLAs

"Build My Life" by New Song Cafe
https://www.youtube.com/watch?v=oriF6-ws_kU

"Say The Word" by Hillsong United
https://www.youtube.com/watch?v=HljohpgBrWE

Books:
The Power of One Christlike Life by Francis Frangipane
What God Really Thinks About Women by Sharon Jaynes

NOTES

Chapter 2

1. Warren Wiersbe, *Be Authentic, (Colorado Springs, Co: David C. Cook), 69.*

Chapter 3

1. For more on heart healing, visit Freedom In Christ Ministries at ficm.org
2. Eric Ludy, Https://ellerslie.com/bravehearted-christian

Chapter 4

Chapter 5

1. Emphasis added.
2. Emphasis added.

Chapter 6

Chapter 7

1. Emphasis added.

Chapter 8

1. Moms In Prayer International, https://momsinprayer.org
2. The Pulse Movement, https://pulsemovement.com

Chapter 9

1. Oswald Chambers, https://utmost.org/the-cross-in-prayer/
2. E. M. Bounds, *Prayer and Praying Men*, (George H. Doran Company), 17.

Chapter 10

1. Emphasis added.
2. Emphasis added.

ABOUT

the author

I am seriously passionate about moving you, my sisters, into deeper intimacy with God. Through prayer (obviously that is at the top of the topic!) through knowing Him more, and through reminding you that YOU ARE MADE FOR BEAUTIFUL THINGS — Dear friend, no dream is too crazy when God is with you in it.

I love to talk about the journey — how God sees us as who we are becoming, not as we are. His grace is incredibly generous and good and He wants you to enjoy Him while you are shining your light — doing the good works He created you to do before He hung the stars in place.

I have a bazillion stories about God and His amazing love by now. I think this is why it took so long to prep me for His gig. Saving up stories so I could spill them through the spoken word and through writing.

To find out more about my speaking and to book me for your next event, visit www.kathyschwanke.com.

Follow me on all the socials: @kathyschwanke